CHALLENGING ADULT ILLITERACY

Reading and Writing Disabilities in the British Army

CHALLENGING ADULT ILLITERACY

Reading and Writing Disabilities in the British Army

COLIN STEVENSON

TEACHERS COLLEGE PRESS

Teachers College, Columbia University
New York and London

Published by Teachers College Press, 1234 Amsterdam Avenue, New York, N.Y. 10027

Grateful acknowledgment is made to Professor Ben D. Wood and International Business Machines Corporation for their generous grants that made publication of this book possible.

Library of Congress Cataloging in Publication Data

Stevenson, Colin.
Challenging adult illiteracy.

Bibliography: p.
Includes index.
1. Soldiers—Education, Non-military—Great Britain.
2. Reading (Adult education)—Great Britain.
3. Literacy—Great Britain. I. Title.
U717.G7S83 1985 374'.012'0941 85-12603

ISBN 0-8077-2737-7

Manufactured in the United States of America

88 87 86 85 1 2 3 4 5 6

Contents

Foreword

I was pleased when Colin Stevenson asked me to write the Foreword to his book because I remember well the time when his deep interest in the education of the backward adult took root. We first met as long ago as 1953 and became good friends, sharing a common interest in a number of different subjects. At about the same time he introduced me to his wife and family; anyone who has the privilege of their friendship and has enjoyed the happy and humane atmosphere of their family circle will readily understand Colin's devotion to his subject. To have achieved the eminence he has reached in his particular field needs patience, tolerance, hard work, and a sound appreciation of human values. Colin and his family are lucky enough to possess all these characteristics, and it was from this secure and contented background that a real interest in his subject was free to develop and flourish so successfully.

Some years after joining the Army, Colin was posted to the Army School of Education at Beaconsfield where I was Commandant. It was here that he first became drawn to the subject of backwardness among adults, and although there was no opportunity to study raw material, students of the School being candidates for entry into the Royal Army Educational Corps and of a high educational calibre therefore, he nevertheless began serious reading and first became aware of the specific problem of dyslexia and its association with the more general problems of backwardness as a whole. This was an aspect of his subject that he took much farther at a later date. Two years later I was fortunate enough to be in a position to see that he was posted to the School of Preliminary Education where he could give full rein to the study of all aspects of his chosen subject. He spent a total of six years on the staff of the school and during this time embarked on serious research in association with the University of Southampton.

In the first chapter of his book Colin describes the long history of the Army's concern and interest in remedial education. From a purely military point of view this interest was initially restricted; in an Army that was rapidly becoming mechanized and more technical as was the British Army in the 1930s, a soldier whose knowledge of reading and writing was defective was of little use to his unit. The first military interest therefore was restricted to teaching him these two skills. What may be a matter of surprise to those unacquainted with the comprehensiveness of Army training is that the purely technical task of teaching a man to read and write slowly grew into a much broader business involving an appreciation on the part of instructors of the related psychological, educational, and sociological problems. I first saw this happening in its earliest stages, as a very young officer, in one of the two units raised in the 1930s that were named "Educational and Physical Development Depots." In that time of serious unemployment, when many young men suffered from malnutrition, the Army was compelled to recruit men who were not only educationally backward but who were also below the required medical standard. The teaching staffs of these Depots were drawn from personnel of the Royal Army Medical Corps, the Army Educational Corps, and the Army Physical Training Corps. These teachers very quickly recognized the inadequacy of working separately in their own water-tight compartments and began to work closely together in order to compare notes of progress among their students, and particularly did they recognize the need to find out as much as possible about the history of each student's background. This was the embryonic stage of remedial education, but sufficient was being done to give me an acute interest in the importance of and the necessity for a broad approach to this form of instruction. The purely educational need was greatly intensified on the expansion of the Army at the outbreak of the Second World War and subsequently during the period of compulsory National Service in postwar years.

There is no need for me to enlarge upon the more recent history of the tremendous progress made in the context of teaching methods employed in remedial education in the Army; nor to occupy space in recording the extent and depth of research into the whole subject of backwardness among soldiers. Colin has already done both brilliantly in his book, which in itself is an important manifestation of the progress made and, not least, a record of his own valuable contribution. What ought to be noted, however, is the wisdom of the Army Board in recognizing that the scope of remedial education was a much wider matter than the mere teaching of illiterate and semi-literate soldiers to read and write and also in their provision of training time (though the educationists were never satisfied with the amount given!) to enable the Army's Educational Service to achieve so much success. A further point to be made is that the work of the Royal Army Educational Corps has proved to be of immense value to the civilian educational world where much of the teaching practice employed in the School of Preliminary Education has been adopted in state schools. This is especially important for the sake of continuity because the Army has recently found it possible to dispense with its own school on account of the Army's greatly reduced establishment, the cessation of compulsory National Service, and the consequent ability to pick and choose recruits who measure up to the standards, educational and otherwise, that the Army requires. It is good to know, therefore, that the valuable work done by the Army (particularly in the field of research) will not be lost to the nation. By the adoption of similar methods in state schools we can look forward to fewer adolescents leaving school annually with a record of failure behind them. Today's need of a well-educated society that can understand and live comfortably and usefully in an increasingly technological world is greater than ever. There is no place for drop-outs. The understanding of the educational, psychological, and sociological problems involved in overcoming the disadvantages of backwardness at all levels is as important today as ever it was. This I believe to be the fundamental message of Colin Stevenson's book, and I hope it will be read and found useful by all those teachers who are employed in fighting against the evils and dangers of backwardness.

Major General (Ret) E. F. Foxton
CB, OBE, MA (Oxon), Dip. Ed.(Oxon)

1 Introduction

In the War in which we are engaged, no man can pretend to say how long it will last.

WELLINGTON

HISTORICAL BACKGROUND

In the field of remedial adult education the British Army has a long and honorable history that began as early as 1643 with the issuance of a series of pocket books, of which the best known is the Soldiers' Pocket Bible. Military Schools have existed since the birth of the Regular Army in 1660, and the evidence suggests that their efforts were divided equally between the troops and the children, a pattern that persisted until 1914. In 1846 a Royal Warrant established the Corps of Army Schoolmasters, entry to which was open only to those who had received training in teaching methods. The members of this Corps were engaged during the day in teaching the children in Army Schools and during the evening in combating the problems of illiteracy among soldiers. This task they performed with considerable distinction until the formation of the Army Educational Corps in 1920. Reliable statistics on the extent of illiteracy and semi-illiteracy in the Army during this period are, unfortunately, not available. In 1926, however, the introduction of recruiting tests that placed a man in one of five grades, A to E, began to yield reliable figures, and it is those concerning grades D and E that are of interest in the context of this study. Grade D was used to classify those men who could do no more than read and write a few simple words and who were familiar with the application of the four rules of number. Recruits graded E were below that standard, and their chances of remaining in the Army depended ultimately upon the level of recruitment.

In 1935, 25,000 men were recruited, of whom 6,000 were graded D, and 2,300 were graded E, together representing 33.2 percent of the annual intake. During the 12-year period 1926–38 the total percentage of recruits graded D and E was never lower than 25 percent of the annual recruitment. At the time of Munich the percentage was 24, subdivided between groups D and E in a ratio of 2:1. It is hardly surprising, therefore, that Col. A. C. T. White, VC, (1963) in his book, *The Story of Army Education,* writes: "Every prewar member of the Corps was familiar with the problems of the illiterate." Thus, through the years, individual instructors in Army Education had acquired considerable knowledge of the problem of teaching the functionally illiterate adult, but this pool of knowledge and experience was as yet uncoordinated.

The real impetus to the organization of special courses to meet the needs of educationally substandard recruits did not come until after the outbreak of World War II. It then became apparent that among the vast army of conscripted men, many were functioning well below their innate capacities and many others would be unable to assimilate their normal military training without some form of educational therapy. Thus, at one of the most critical periods in British history the Army found itself in a position where, unless some effective measures were taken, not only would there be an enormous waste of potential within the training organization but there would also be many recruits whose chances of being retained in the service would be marginal.

Commencing in 1940 a number of Army commands organized educational courses that emphasized reading and writing, and also contained elements of practical usefulness and interest, such as household repairs and gardening. Not until 1943, however, was the problem of the functionally illiterate recruit tackled on a coordinated and organized Army-wide basis. The Army Council then authorized the establishment of Basic Education Centres, and recruits attended these as a result of personnel selection tests and sometimes of psychiatric screening. It was decreed that the maximum number in a class should not exceed 15 and the curriculum should not include more than 4 hours per day on elementary literacy skills. To assist those instructors who were engaged in this therapeutic exercise, the Army Education Service produced an English textbook, *English Parade.* Thus, the importance of simple communication skills to the soldier was at last officially recognized; implicit in this recognition was the connection between working literacy and morale. This action set the basic pattern in Britain, both within and outside the Army, for the growth of remedial education as we know it today.

The Basic Education Centre of the war years not only made a significant contribution to the size of the pool of "trainable" manpower, and to morale, but also set the stage for the expansion of this service in the immediate postwar era. At the end of the war the older men were gradually released from the Service and replaced by a new phenomenon, the National Service conscript. Writing of these men, Colonel White (1963) states:

> More than twenty per cent of these recruits were nearly illiterate and two per cent wholly so, the incidence varying from arm to arm; the 'problem case' was almost non-existent in the Royal Armoured Corps, and was abundantly evident in the Royal Pioneer Corps, one unit commander of which reported in 1946 that forty per cent of his men could not write a simple letter without help.

While the problem was still very much in evidence, however, the causative factors were very different. The educationally backward prewar recruit had frequently been exposed to very little schooling, but his postwar counterpart was the product of a generation whose life and schooling had been disrupted by evacuations, air raids, an acute shortage of teaching staff, and all the multifarious inconveniences of war-time existence.

The *Interim Scheme of General Education in the Army* was published in 1946, and this established, on the pattern set by the Basic Education Centres, Preliminary Education Centres (PEC) in each command to provide courses for National Servicemen and Regular soldiers. These Centres, staffed by R.A.E.C. officers, warrant officers, and sergeants, provided 6-week courses. There were 20 men in each intake every 2 weeks. The 1947 *General Education Handbook* suggested the following allocation of student time in a preliminary education course: 50 percent to "Reading and Writing," 12.5 percent to "Citizenship and News," 12.5 percent to "Physical Training and Games," and only 7.5 percent to "Arithmetic." In 1951 a new five-year regular engagement was introduced, and the vacancies on PEC courses were reserved for the new regular recruits. The PEC contribution to Army manpower during this period is summed up by Colonel White:

> Eighty per cent of those attending attained a level of literacy that not only made them trainable, but improved their powers of social adjustment. It was claimed that the Centres saved each year the equivalent of a brigade, by reclaiming men who otherwise would inevitably have been discharged. (1963, p. 182)

Despite the valuable contribution made by the Preliminary Education Centres, it was evident that a six-week course had serious limitations; besides, very small, highly-specialized units are beset with organizational problems. It was decided, in the interest of efficiency and economy, that remedial education would be provided in a central establishment. At the end of 1956, therefore, the PEC were consolidated into the School of Preliminary Education (SPE) at Everleigh, near Tidworth, and in 1957 nearly 1,000 soldiers attended its courses. In 1959 the school moved to Perham Down where it remained until midsummer 1962, when it moved to the excellent barracks at Hawthorne, Wiltshire. The story of the SPE during the 1960s was one of constant pressures to cut costs, and indeed for a while there was some danger of abolition. At the end of 1965 the 12-week course was reduced to 10½ weeks, and the maximum number in a class raised from 14 to 17. The reshaping of a much-reduced Regular Army cut the school's annual enrollment to 500 men, and in consequence, the intakes were rearranged to arrive every 3 weeks instead of every 2. This reshaping further changed the role of the school. The recruits were different both from the prewar unschooled men and from the immediate postwar soldiers suffering from war-time disruption of their environment. The School was now required to motivate, and to modify the attitudes of young soldiers who had failed to respond to the educational opportunities previously provided—a far more demanding task.

At the time of the study reported in this book the School of Preliminary Education was a unique establishment. Britain had no other comparable civilian or military institution where an average of 110 resident adults were undergoing full-time remedial education. The school continued in existence until 1981 because the Army, to fulfill its many commitments, still found it necessary to accept recruits who were potentially good soldiers, but whose educational standards were too low to enable them to assimilate the complex training required for the modern Army. Some 10 percent of recruits came within this category, and the majority were infantrymen.

AIM

The aim of the school, as defined in the School Charter shown in Appendix A, was

> To provide a 10½ week course for those soldiers who require tuition to raise them to the educational standard necessary to enable them to

> benefit fully from normal training and to fit them to carry out the duties of their Arms or Corps. By improvement of their skills in reading, writing and number, they will be encouraged and given the opportunity to reach the highest standards of which they are capable as trained soldiers, tradesmen and potential leaders.

In simple terms the school existed to help make soldiers out of men who would otherwise be unacceptable. While the school was therefore an integral part of the training organization of the Army, the work had an undoubted welfare and citizenship value. The nature of this task can perhaps be better appreciated when it is realized how very little was known in civilian education about the remedial education of adults. No common doctrine of general approach or experience of teaching methods existed that could be adapted to military requirements. There was a dearth of suitable reading material and teaching aids, and all these problems had to be solved within the school by trial and error.

SELECTION OF STUDENTS

Recruits were eligible for a course at the school if their selection group ratings were below a prescribed minimum. They were eligible if they had a reading age lower than 11 years or if they had a significant weakness in mathematics. The selection was carried out by the school, and approximately 34 students assembled every 3 weeks. The school's facilities provided for a maximum of 136 students at any one time and a yearly turnover of approximately 500.

ORGANIZATION

Every intake of 34 students was divided into two classes, each with its own officer instructor who remained with the group through the entire course. As part of the induction procedure, students were given a series of objective group tests under the control of the testing and diagnostic officer. The test scores were studied by the instructors who had freedom to arrange the classes as seemed best suited to the general requirement. When dealing with such small numbers, it was not practicable to lay down any rigid set of rules or division into classes—streaming in its usual sense was not possible, even if it had been desirable. It was sometimes possible, however, to form a group of "bright" students, just as it was necessary to form one of men who were particularly backward in reading or math. The course program was arranged so that, at any one time, there were three intakes at varying stages of the course. In addition, there were two small remedial classes for the most backward readers who were taken from the normal classes, and for this special instruction the staffing ratio was 1:8. The course timetable included periods of drill, physical education, games, religious instruction, and hobbies. Actual educational instruction amounted to about 20 hours per week, and for this there were no set syllabi or standardized lessons. How this time was spent was largely in the hands of each instructor who worked on the premise that every student presented a particular problem that must be diagnosed and dealt with individually.

TESTING AND RESEARCH

Objective group tests were administered to all students at the beginning and end of their course. Further tests were utilized by instructors to assist them with individual diagnosis. General supervision and control of testing procedures was exercised by the testing and diagnostic officer who also administered more elaborate individual tests in the diagnosis of difficult cases. The main purpose of the school tests, however, was not so much to measure improvement in attainment as to provide graded material that, when carefully analyzed, could be a valuable indicator of disabilities and learning gaps. The school engaged in research and experimental work as far as resources permitted. It was regarded as important that research projects be undertaken that involved the use of differing methods and media, to prevent teaching methods from degenerating into dull repetition, and also to formulate new ideas and new methods in this unique teaching situation.

This, then, is the background to this study, which was designed to create an overall picture of the type of student found at the School of Preliminary Education; to establish the causes of his educational backwardness and to relate these to linguistic performance; and to compare the effectiveness of the approaches and methods used to alleviate his disabilities.

2 The Nature of the Problem

The harvest truly is plenteous, but the labourers are few.

ST. MATTHEW

This chapter examines briefly the overall situation in the United Kingdom regarding backwardness in reading. The reader will then be better able to assess the Army's considerable contribution in combating this problem.

DEFINING LITERACY

In any discussion of reading standards, it is necessary to define exactly what is meant by the term *backwardness.* In the officially accepted standards, as defined by the Department of Education and Science (DES) and described in the Ministry of Education (1950) Pamphlet No. 18, an illiterate has "a reading age less than 7 years," and a semi-illiterate, "a reading age less than 9 years but not less than 7 years." In real terms, however, I do not think that these criteria are relevant any longer to the requirements of daily life in this technological era. An adequate facility in that aspect of human communication called reading is a basic requisite of life in a civilized society. Reading enters into the personal, social, and economic life of every citizen.

In this context, therefore, I am concerned not merely with the mechanics of reading, the translating of symbols into meaningful sounds, but *reading with understanding*—the understanding necessary to obtain information for the everyday business of living. We need to establish as a common aim the sensible and practical definition of literacy set out in the *Newsom Report* (Ministry of Education, 1963):

> Literacy involves the power to invest words with meaning, to recognise the ideas which somebody else wishes them to convey and to use them oneself to express the thoughts which without their help, would remain fleeting and inchoate.

We are living in an age when the emphasis in employment is shifting strongly in favor of highly trained people working in professional and technical occupations; an age when there is an increasing requirement for mobility of labor and retraining schemes. A further byproduct of the technological revolution is the massive increase in leisure time because of automation and reduced working hours. All these factors are having an increasing impact upon the personal and social lives and attitudes of the population.

If we are to avoid the consequences of boredom, apathy, restlessness, and nihilism in the form of delinquent behavior in our society, there is little place for those whose reading ability is the mouthing of sounds with no real understanding. Standards of reading need to be related to society's fundamental demands, which are becoming ever more complex. A country cannot afford, either economically or psychologically, large numbers of its population with a disability that is likely to be both an occupational and social handicap for the rest of their lives.

My experience with soldiers at the School of Preliminary Education has convinced me that, to cope adequately with the everyday demands of living, those with a reading age of 12 years or less must be regarded as functionally illiterate. The importance of general social literacy cannot be over-emphasized, and this aspect is stressed in the *Newsom Report*:

> One of the reasons why there is a quite proper anxiety over the general standards of literacy today is not that fewer and fewer people can read and write, but that more and more people need to do so with greater competence.

The majority of the SPE soldiers came within this functionally illiterate category. They had some knowledge and ability in reading and simple calculations, but it was a knowledge from which they derived no enjoyment nor satisfaction. In most cases their previous employment did not require any continued practice of these arts, and the little skill that had been acquired at school was soon dissipated.

EXTENT OF FUNCTIONAL ILLITERACY

It is extremely difficult to make any precise pronouncements on the extent of functional illiteracy in an adult population. Unless those in this category become caught up in the probation service, approved schools, prisons, family service units, or industrial rehabilitation units, the extent of the problem remains concealed. In addition, this is a disability about which the majority are secretive and sensitive since it carries an unfortunate social stigma. Many are not only shy and embarrassed but suffer feelings of guilt.

The results of a survey organized by the National Association for Remedial Education (1972) showed that in England and Wales, excluding training centers and penal institutions, approximately 200 centers were providing instruction for about 2,800 nonimmigrant and 1,400 immigrant illiterates. This, however, was merely a ripple on the surface of a very deep pond. The same survey showed that of the 166 county and county boroughs in England and Wales, only 104 regularly provided such instruction. Fourteen authorities made no provision whatsoever, 21 offered facilities if requested, and 27 apparently regarded the matter as being of such little importance that they did not see fit to reply to the survey.

It is obvious from these figures that many medium-sized towns in England and Wales made no provision for the adult backward reader and also that only a very small proportion of those who could have benefitted from remedial assistance received it. A further factor that militated against a successful approach to this problem was the insistence of many Local Education Authorities (LEAs) on a minimum number of students before allowing another education class to be established. This difficulty was exacerbated in many cases by further prohibitory regulations stating that if attendance fell below 75 percent for three consecutive meetings, the class should be closed. Obviously there must be strict financial control over further education expenditure, as over any other public funds. It is nevertheless regrettable that this particular problem was approached in so many instances on exactly the same financial and educational basis as leisure activity classes, thus indicating a wide-ranging lack of appreciation of the nature of the disability and its attendant difficulties. However, following the appointment of Sir Alan Bullock as Chairman of a Government Committee of Inquiry into Reading and the Use of English, there was a substantial increase in the number of LEAs attempting the necessary provision, and also restrictive practices governing tutor/student ratios were abandoned. This information was gathered through questionnaires returned to the British Council for the Rehabilitation of the Disabled Working Party on The Dyslexic Adult.

The most disturbing and indeed alarming figures on the extent of adult functional illiteracy were those presented to the above Working Party by the Inner London Education Authority (ILEA, 1969). A survey of the Authority's day-release classes carried out by the Authority's inspectors in 13 colleges of further education, not including any technical colleges, revealed these broad classifications:

Reading Age 8 years or less	3.6 percent
Reading Age 9 years	24.8 percent
Reading Age 10 years	33.0 percent

If the DES reading standards are applied in this situation, we then have 28.4 percent who are semi-illiterate; a further 4.6 percent are barely above this threshold, possess levels of reading skills easily lost without practice, and certainly do not meet the Newsom criteria of literacy. The evidence also drew attention to the fact that the 28.4 percent semi-illiterates included many whose problems were so severe that they could not be solved within a normal classroom situation. In some colleges it was necessary to set up special classes for those students whose literacy skills did not match their ability in other fields.

These facts were sufficiently alarming on their own, but they did not present the complete, depressing picture. The figures quoted did not take into account the proportions of backward readers among those employed in unskilled manual occupations or among the immigrant population; neither of these featured in any significant numbers in day-release groups.

It may be argued that the figures in the ILEA Survey (1969) were produced by the peculiar socio-economic skew of the capital city. The number of LEAs that have conducted similar surveys is not known; most were markedly reluctant to discuss this subject. I was given to understand by the ILEA, however, that a similar study undertaken in Bradford, but including those in technical colleges and the immigrant populations, had produced similar findings. In fact, reading experts are agreed that surveys in any of the major metropolitan areas would produce similar or worse data.

The situation, therefore, should give rise to serious concern not only to the educational profession but also to all those concerned with the quality of human life and employment in our society. One may only speculate on the numbers whose training potential is restricted and whose employment promotion prospects are inhibited by a lack of literacy skills. It is tempting also to speculate to what degree this unfortunate situation influences patterns of employment, job fall-out, and the creation of "drifters" in our society. To what extent is this failure of our educational system responsible for the frustration, the stresses and strains created by unfulfilled lives, which often lead to antisocial behavior?

Some answers to this question indicating positive links to such behavior are to be found in later chapters; it is also interesting to note that Martin Wright, Secretary of the Howard League for Penal Reform (1971), wrote: "remedial classes have to be provided for 25 percent of juvenile offenders in institutions." As has been outlined in the previous chapter, the British Army has considerable experience in this particular field and has made determined progress in its efforts to combat the problems. From 1965 to 1975 the percentage of men joining the Army in need of remedial education fluctuated between 8 and 12 percent. In 1975 the Directorate of Army Education stated the figure to be approximately 8 percent. Although this is significantly lower than either the 34 percent at the time of Munich or 25 percent during National Service after World War II, it cannot be assumed that this in any way reflected greatly improved national standards of reading. The sole reason for the difference is that the over-all standards required for a recruit for the volunteer army of the 70s were considerably higher than those required at the time of national emergency in 1938 and during compulsory National Service. The survey of reading attainment undertaken during the period of National Service, and contained in the *Crowther Report* (Ministry of Education, 1960), presented an accurate picture of the over-all situation regarding adult literacy. The ILEA Survey (1969) would appear to indicate that the figure of 25 percent obtained from the National Service survey reflected the extent of the problem on a national basis.

The hypothesis that adult literacy mirrors the standards achieved in the school system is supported from two sources. The evidence from the DES (1966) Survey indicates that in 1964 standards of 15-year-old pupils were nearly 2 years in advance of the standards that similar pupils attained in 1948. However, a comparison of the 1948 results with the standards obtained in 1938 shows them to be 1½ years lower. It is probable that the 1948 results had been depressed by evacuation of children, call-up of teachers for military service, and general disruption during the war years. The improvement acclaimed in the DES Survey as "a striking record of progress" was, to a large extent, illusory. Start and Wells (1972) analyzed the National Survey of Reading Comprehension undertaken in 1970–71 by the National Foundation for Educational Research (NFER) at the request of the Department of Education and Science. They concluded: "At the end we are faced with the fact that reading standards today are no better than they were a decade ago." These are disturbing thoughts since we have already shown that standards in 1964 were not an improvement on those obtained in 1938. In data published in the *Journal of the Association of Educational Psychologists* (1969) Burt went further and suggested that there had been no real improvement in standards of literacy since the second decade of this century.

It is no longer possible to blame the war, call-up, or evacuation, as disruptive factors. Further education classes are not solely composed of the middle-aged, whose schooling was subject to war-time disruption. According to the 1972 survey by the National Association for Remedial Education, 50 percent of students attending classes for backward/illiterate adults left school within the preceding five years. Thus again the pieces fit the same pattern as the evidence from the ILEA Survey (1969).

It is therefore worthwhile to examine the evidence provided by other research concerning both the standards and the teaching of reading in our schools. One of the most important surveys was by Morris (1966) in the Kent schools. In the introduction to this work, Wall writes: "30% of 15 year olds could be classified as backward readers, semi-illiterate and illiterate in 1952." When studying the findings, it is important to note that ability in the Kent schools was above the national norm. Nevertheless, in the first year after the infant/junior transfer stage, Morris found 45 percent of 7,000 children still in need of infant materials and methods. Of those children in the 1946-age groups who had been classified as "poor" readers, 65 percent were found to be still backward and 1½ percent semi-illiterate/illiterate when retested in the fourth year of junior school. On a further follow-up at the school-leaving age, 47 percent were still backward, 8 percent were semi-illiterate, and 21 percent were unable to read above the standard of 11-year-olds. On a book criterion test fewer than 16 percent of those previously classified as "poor" readers had a reading level commensurate with their chronological age in the year in which they reached school-leaving age.

Perhaps even more telling are the figures concerning knowledge of the teaching of reading. Of the teachers of the 7,000 mentioned above,

1. 75 percent had no training in infant methods
2. 52 percent had no infant school experience

3. 18 percent admitted they had no knowledge of how to teach the skill of reading

Even in 1971 a survey by Gerald Platt of the Manchester Teachers' Centre indicated no room for complacency in this area. From teachers trained at 48 colleges as far apart as Northumberland, London, York, and Ireland, Platt sought opinions of their college training in the teaching of reading. The results were as follows:

1. 35 percent had no training in this subject whatsoever
2. 35 percent considered the limited training they received poor
3. 19 percent considered the training they received only fair

Platt (1971) also found that the vast majority of schools still relied solely on word recognition tests. In only three schools was comprehension tested, which appears to indicate that the whole purpose of reading had not been appreciated.

Gardner (1968) studied trends in early reading standards in the junior schools of a Midland area from 1961 to 1967. In 1961 he found that one in four of first-year primary school pupils in his sample of 2,000 had not started learning to read. This proportion increased annually until it reached 40 percent in 1967.

Gardner's findings supported those of the National Child Development (NCD) Survey (1966), which showed that "about 45% appear not to reach full mastery of reading skills by the time they are due to leave infant schools." Thus this survey supported the 1953 findings of Morris (1966). The NCD Survey also revealed disquieting behavioral problems associated with lack of school progress. It was found that 13 percent of 7-year-olds were already showing signs of behavioral "maladjustment." Approximately one in ten of the children had already been referred to some outside agency because of behavior difficulties or lack of progress. The report further stated: "A minimum of 5% have quite serious adjustment problems while at least a further 10% show stress symptoms of various kinds."

The NCD Study (1966) highlighted the need for teachers to be adequately trained in reading skills and in the recognition and diagnosis of learning difficulties; other research showed this need to be at odds with reality. The ILEA *Literacy Survey* (1969) showed that fewer than one in eight of the full-time teachers of junior classes had been trained to teach reading. Overall, 63 percent of junior schools or junior departments had no full-time teacher who had received any specific instruction in the teaching of reading during his or her professional training.

This acute shortage of teachers adequately trained to teach reading in junior schools and departments is the thin end of an alarming wedge. The practice in colleges of education has been for students training for infant and infant/junior groups to receive considerably more instruction in the teaching of reading than those preparing for employment in junior and secondary schools or departments. In evidence presented to the James Committee of Inquiry into Teacher Training, Southgate (1971) reported an investigation of one area that showed students training for infants or infant/junior groups received an average of 12 hours of instruction in teaching early stages of reading. In some colleges it was considerably less. The time allocation for those preparing for junior teaching varied from 1 to 6 hours and for junior/secondary trainees from zero to 3 hours. It is hardly surprising, therefore, that a Manchester Inspector of Schools was quoted in the (London) *Times Educational Supplement* as stating that illiteracy was a serious problem that was becoming much worse. He also stated that tests administered in 12 comprehensive schools showed that one-third of the students were below-average readers and that, in some schools, the proportion was 45 percent.

The plight is severe, therefore, for those children who find difficulty in beginning to read, or those who have reached the secondary education stage while still backward in this vital subject. Brennan (1971), ILEA Inspector of Special Education, estimated that about one-third of county boroughs and one-half of county LEAs had made only a start in the provision of effective remedial services, and that the best of these only approached one-half of the necessary provision.

The situation has been exacerbated by the fact that remedial teaching has been obsessed with reading schemes to the detriment of individual development. Remedial education cannot be divorced from the requirement for overall therapy. Besides, teachers have long regarded the remedial service as low-grade employment; in consequence, it has not always attracted teachers of the necessary caliber, experience, and professional expertise.

To the disturbing facts on reading attainment and the training of reading teachers must be added a related factor concerning the increasing incidence of truancy. At a conference of the National Association of Chief Education Officers' Welfare Officers in Bournemouth on May 22, 1973, the CEO for Southampton stated that there were 500,000 truants. The indications are that we have been too complacent about attendance records; the revealing concentrations of absence have been ignored. Wiseman (1968) found a significant relationship between school attainment and attendance, and increasing truancy will, therefore, exacerbate the existing problem of backwardness in reading.

CONCLUSIONS

Although no detailed nor accurate nation-wide figures were available on the number of functionally illiterate adults, an examination of the reading standards in our school system showed a fairly constant general picture: some 20–25 percent of the secondary school population were at least 2 years behind their chronological age in reading ability. The research indicated this in itself to be a reflection of the disturbing standards in many of our junior schools and an indictment of the provision for training teachers in reading and language development.

Adult literacy is a product of the standards achieved in our schools. The findings relating to reading attainment among school children are reflected in the limited evidence that is available concerning the adult population. In effect a distressingly large element of the population has been prevented from operating efficiently, and the resultant frustrations and limitations produce a disadvantaged, depressed, and perhaps embittered element in our society.

For those students who are backward at the time of transfer to the junior school system, the prognosis for adult life is not attractive. That their ultimate disability can be alleviated by well organized effort and sympathetic understanding of their problem is shown by the efforts of some official and voluntary bodies; and in particular by the investigation detailed in the following chapters.

3 The School

It is wrong to coerce people into opinions, but it is our duty to impel them into experience.

KURT HAHN

This chapter discusses the basic philosophy of the School of Preliminary Education and the principles that formed the basis of its teaching doctrine. It is important, however, that these be viewed in the perspective of the aim of the school charter, as set out in Chapter 1, and the fact that the school's fundamental purpose was to assist in producing a more mature, responsible soldier capable of thinking for himself and acting on his own initiative.

The young men concerned were prepared for an adult role in society. Most were victims of an education that stressed success in terms of academic achievement at the expense of an understanding of responsible citizenship. The SPE attempted to turn these young men into adults, to give them a real identity in place of the rejection previously encountered at home, in school, and consequently in society. Many had joined the Army sadly disillusioned by their experiences in the civilian labor market where, as the standards of living rose, new and more complex demands were made upon workers, who in turn needed to be better educated and more adaptable. It may well be that for these men of less than average ability the transition from school to community life was too abrupt and too difficult because of an academically biased curriculum. They had, therefore, a need to belong, to feel part of a community, since one area of their failure was social adaptation—an inability to establish adequate personal relationships, coupled with a marked lack of confidence when faced with new situations.

Problems of social maladjustment, a feature in the lives of many of these men, are examined in detail in Chapter 4. Since, however, these same problems provide overtones that were echoed in the tenor of life at the school, it is necessary to state briefly that many were resolved or considerably alleviated on, or soon after, enlistment. The man, in making the important decision to join the Army, found a home and a sense of security. The Army became a father figure that made his personal decisions in addition to feeding and clothing him to a high standard. He made friends and, probably for the first time in his life, learned to identify with a social group constituted by his unit, corps, or regiment, and the Army as a whole.

THE EDUCATIONAL PROBLEMS

The educational problems posed by these soldiers were principally with backwardness in reading, comprehension, and spelling, and to a lesser extent with backwardness in arithmetic. The greatest problem was that of arousing motivation. While aware of their educational failings, the students who attended SPE arrived with widely differing attitudes. They fell into three broad categories:

1. Those who resented and resisted education because it reactivated their sense of failure and feelings of inferiority
2. Those who welcomed the opportunity afforded to them but had very serious doubts about their own abilities to succeed
3. Those who had no sense of failure and were satisfied with their low standard of attainment

Each of these groups posed a separate problem. The first two groups needed the reassurance that they could succeed, and situations had to be contrived through which they could experience the encouragement of progress and success and the beginnings of a new self-respect. The third group had to be led to a reappraisal of standards and encouraged to greater efforts. However, all these men required awakening in some measure to the world around them and represented a constant challenge to the skill and imagination of the instructor.

It is obvious that in 10½ weeks the school could not remedy the inadequacies that remained after 10 years of schooling. It is equally certain that for adult students whose educational disabilities have been caused or aggravated by personality maladjustment, any form of academic approach can only serve to reinforce their sense of failure and frustration. These men arrived at the SPE because they had failed to keep pace with the ordinary school curriculum in this type of education.

In this context therefore the aim of the school may appear overambitious. However, the school was not attempting the educationally impossible but was making a determined effort to produce responsible adults who would be able to work effectively within an ordered framework.

THE APPROACH TO REMEDIAL INSTRUCTION

In considering the overall aim of the SPE, it is obvious that, to achieve any degree of success with these men, a fresh approach to their inseparable educational and social problems would be required. In analyzing this approach, we must consider the actual physical environment, the organization, the role of the instructor, and the curriculum.

The Environment

The school's physical environment had considerable advantages. It was located in beautiful countryside some 7 miles east of Bath and built of Bath stone. The facade, the structure, and the conditions were the envy of visitors from a very wide variety of educational institutions. The student was, therefore, placed immediately in an environment that was not only admirable for its purpose but also singularly attractive in its landscaped grounds. The quality of these surroundings helped the students to accept an educational environment. The very appearance of the school immediately allayed some of the misgivings and anxiety they might have felt upon arrival. In many cases the school was the most pleasant environment they had ever experienced, and they were very ready to say so; for example, "If I'd lived in a place like this instead of five in a room with no bathroom and no garden I don't reckon I'd 'ave been here now!" They appreciated the atmosphere, and that was the first step toward an acceptance of the overall educational therapy.

The Organization

The SPE was part of the Army Training Organization and was, therefore, run as a military unit, with a regimental headquarters, controlling both training and administration, and two training wings. The school was commanded by a Lieutenant Colonel, RAEC, assisted by a Major, RAEC, who was both deputy commandant and chief instructor and was responsible for the educational and administrative aspects of instruction. While this type of organization does have distinct advantages in that there is no constant battle over discipline, it could, if the authority were used arbitrarily, have an abrasive effect and reinforce feelings of antipathy and resentment—a conflict between Mars and Minerva. The school did, I think, successfully integrate and balance the requirements of normal military discipline with an understanding of the educational rehabilitation process to produce an authority that was not striving to control and not repressive; an authority that also gave freedom—and the students learned from the difference.

It may well be that these men had only experienced school systems in which authority had been used in a defensive role, thereby creating hostility, aggressiveness, and apathy. Such are the educational systems of which Farley (1960) writes: "Ninety per cent of the work in a Secondary Modern School is control and discipline."

Organization is a vitally important aspect of remedial education, as Taylor (1949) discussed in *Experiments with a Backward Class.* The military organization of the SPE ensured the smooth running of day-to-day affairs; obtaining and maintaining supplies and equipment; the provision of meals, accommodations, and clothing, and all financial aspects including the students' pay. The fact that the organization was so efficient and so predictable helped considerably in the educational rehabilitation process, for it absolved these men from the need to make decisions inherent in planning daily life. To them the authority was a form of security that engendered a feeling of belonging. They were insecure because of repeated failure and feelings of inadequacy and because for many of them family life, the normal primary source of security, had been the complete antithesis of this. (For a detailed examination of this issue, see Chapter 4.) In addition, many of them never had any sense of belonging during their school life because of their inadequacy in the academic world. The controlled and understanding authority of the SPE lessened emotional stress, and they looked upon the Army as a source of protection. Thus the military organization made the man feel part of it even though he was inadequate. The sense of comradeship fostered by the environment appeared to compensate in some measure for the lack of feeling of group membership in the family situation.

The Role of the Instructor

In considering the actual approach to remedial instruction within the organization, it is necessary to make some general observations about the student population. Although all these men were educationally backward, they differed widely in achievement in the basic skills. Many, in fact, showed considerable variation of ability within their own attainment profiles. A large number had been considered as educationally subnormal (ESN); although they were not officially classified as such, they felt they had been so labeled. They had experienced the stigma of backwardness because they had not been given the opportunity of being tutored in special classes. It is interesting to record here that being singled out for special help in the Remedial Centre gave the backward a particular type of pride.

A soldier aged 19½ years, unable to register on the Initial Reading Test, later stated:

> This is the best thing that ever happened to me. I'm in this lot because I need proper treatment. Playing with plasticine at the back never done nobody any good, did it? I was thick and stupid THEY said. "You won't never be any good because you're stupid and idle" they said. They wasn't worried that there was five of us in two beds and the old man came home drunk and knocked us all about. It's different here. The Colonel stopped me yesterday and asked me 'ow I was getting on. I told 'im I wrote my first letter. I only been 'ere three and a half weeks and I went to ——— school for ten years! The Colonel called me by my name. THEY called me things I couldn't even tell what they was.

This is an example of the type of men of whom Wall (1946) wrote in an earlier study of reading backwardness in the Army: "The most likely explanation appears, therefore, to be that physical and environmental factors have combined in early years to produce in these men a mental gesture of avoidance when faced with any form of learning."

It is obvious that with such men diagnosis must play an exceedingly important role. The students were given a battery of group tests, described in detail in Chapter 5, and further individual tests as necessary. The importance of diagnosis within subjects cannot be over-stressed. An analysis of faults and difficulties was required. Instructors needed to maintain constant and perceptive observations, to record impressions of character, attitudes, abilities, disabilities, and general progress. They also had to learn to differentiate between the slow, the slow and retarded, and those of high innate ability who had specific learning difficulties.

It was necessary, therefore, to maintain very comprehensive records for each man. Each student had to be studied with care and insight, and an examination made of the whole constellation of circumstances of his life. This was a considerable task for the instructor, but it is the main reason why he was allocated a group of students who remained his particular responsibility during their progress through the school. It was through this constant contact that he rapidly came to be regarded as a guide, counsellor, friend, and father-figure. The extent to which a man in these circumstances would reveal to his "own" instructor his most intimate thoughts and difficulties within a week of arrival never ceased to astonish me. This continuity of relationship with one particular instructor was, I believe, the catalyst in the training. There appears little doubt that an integrated personality was best achieved if the recruit remained with one group and one father-figure.

A 27-year-old soldier commented during an interview:

> You know Captain X. Well, 'e done wonders with me. I never thought I 'ad it in me. He done more for me in 8 weeks than my old man done all my ——— life. He's always talking to me 'elping me. He never says 'Wot you want with that book there you ——— idiot? I always thought you was thick but now I sees you with a book. Think you're a bleeding toff do you?' Captain X he asks me about the books I read and 'ow I like them. 'e tells me about the books he reads and treats me like I'm a real person.

In this type of relationship, however, there was a danger that the instructor had to take care to avoid. Through this constant communication and his desire to achieve success, he could not allow himself to become over-identified with the men's problems. He had to resist the temptation only to give and had to make constant demands upon them. However, he had also to avoid the pitfall of over-demanding and thus causing stress. He was required to understand their frustration and insecurity, but at the same time he could not absolve them from responsibility. He was, in fact, giving constant support and guidance, and there is an enormous strain in maintaining this good rapport. The strain arose not just from the intensity of the actual teaching commitment, from being continually very original and creative in providing genuine individual work, but also from the fact that many of the learning difficulties stemmed from behavioral disturbances and environmental factors. Besides, those who have difficulty in learning often have problems of attention, so that the material had to be broken down into small units and actual "learning" sessions had to be severely restricted. The anxiety that the backward man feels impairs clear thinking and often disturbs the memory process. The majority had many years of learning negative responses, which had become habitual and were not easily modified.

In this context, therefore, it may be seen that the task of the instructor at SPE was probably the most physically and mentally exhausting, but also the most rewarding, in the Army Education Service. Very few indeed had had any previous training in remedial teaching, and in the absence of any body of established knowledge, they acquired their expertise from actual experience and also from the vast fund of expertise that was handed down within the school under the guidance of the chief instructor.

Newsom has drawn attention to the skills required in the teaching of the deprived: "By their very nature these young people require outstanding professional skills and inspiration from those who care for them" (Ministry of Education, 1963). The soldiers were Newsom-type children who had experienced yet further failure and frustration in their attempts at finding satisfactory employment. How much greater, therefore, the skills and understanding required by those responsible for their educational therapy. These instructors had to possess a combination of teaching skills and the approach of the social worker.

The Curriculum

Perhaps the factor that most surprised the many visitors to SPE was that the school operated an educational program without a traditional timetable. Obviously there was a timetable, but it contained only the most basic and absolutely necessary information. Periods of drill, PT, sports, and breaks were marked, but there were no set periods for subject instruction. The object of this system was to ensure the greatest possible flexibility, which allowed the instructor to take advantage of spurts of interest and enthusiasm. Despite the wide disparity of ability within groups, genuine individual and group work could take place at one and the same time.

Cleugh (1968) stated that "What really matters is what goes on in the school or class and the relationship it engenders." What goes on in a class must therefore be organized. Individual and group teaching are only of any value if they are methodical. The fact that no subject timetable existed at SPE did not indicate a lack of method or of organization. The emphasis for each student was shifted from looking for backwardness to looking for abilities. It was vital that each student be able to savor the experience of success in some aspect of the overall therapeutic program, whether at drill, PT, football, or one of the basic academic skills. Effort is very closely related to an individual's estimate of his chances for success, and the experience of actual success causes him to aim at a higher level and assists in the resurrection of his self-confidence.

For this reason, in the SPE situation, students were immediately set goals that, with a little effort, they were able to attain. This was true for both mental and physical tasks. It was vital that they did not lower their sights nor experience morale-sapping conditions through being subjected to failure in tasks beyond their capacity. For them learning was not easy. They could not immediately enjoy learning, and it was only when the subject matter was appropriate and relevant to their particular situation and experience that success would be attained. Practical exercises were geared to situations in which they could readily identify themselves from first-hand experience. The instructors always kept in mind that these men, through their unfortunate experiences, had a very great fear of making mistakes.

Work had to proceed with steady practice using graded material of slowly increasing difficulty. There had to be limited objectives, and it could never be forgotten that their overall difficulties had accumulated for years. Competition and pressure were avoided at all costs, and an attitude of mutual help and cooperation was actively encouraged. An attitude of "the weakest to the wall" would have been fatal to the aim of the school, since one of the students' basic problems was that in the past too few people, often including their own parents, paid little attention to their special requirements.

The flexibility of the timetable allowed a very well-diversified curriculum and enabled the instructor to utilize all available methods and apparatus to cope with the differing abilities within the group. It was not uncommon to find groups of students carrying out tasks in all parts of the school building and grounds. On a wider basis the students applied their newly acquired skills and confidence in situations that had some relationship with the demands of military training and Army life. Courses included a series of expeditions and practical exercises ranging from half-day events to a working week spent away from the unit at camp in either tented or very basic accommodation. The students applied their abilities, knowledge, and experience to problems involving not only themselves but also group living. They learned to evaluate a given situation and to decide for themselves on an appropriate course of action. Thus they came to realize that literacy and communication skills are only the means to an end and not an end in themselves.

Other benefits also derived from these expeditions. The instructors gained new and deeper insights into the men's characters and capabilities, while the students gained considerably in self-confidence and self-reliance. Often the camping expeditions opened a man's eyes to a new concept of life. One man, reared in the middle of the Black Country, stated on his return: "D'you know Sir, that's the first bleeding 'oliday I've ever 'ad! I never known anything like it!"

These expeditions, together with the physical training activities in the curriculum, helped to cement team spirit, quicken reactions, and develop personalities. These are important factors in military training.

Organizing the training program with staggered intakes provided interesting opportunities for peer group influence. The "older" students helped the "new" ones to settle down and also gave them confidence in the value of the training course. This can be particularly beneficial in cases where there is a serious deficiency in literacy skills accompanied by deep feelings of inadequacy and insecurity in the learning situation. In the remedial center an "old" student was overheard giving advice to a very anxious newcomer who had voiced doubts not only about the whole course but especially about his own ability to cope: "You want to think yourself ——— lucky, mate. I bin 'ere for three weeks and it's better than bleeding Butlins* 'cause they *helps* you 'ere!"

As part of the introduction to new experiences, the program provided for extra-mural activities in the evenings with facilities for art, woodwork, pottery, photography, .22 shooting, and so forth. It was hoped that attendance at any one of these activities would increase the men's interest in worthwhile leisure pursuits. Often a student with a long history of educational and employment failure revealed considerable talent in art or crafts, and this could then be used as a fulcrum on which to support the development of his personality and of his literacy skills.

CONCLUSIONS

The SPE curriculum was extremely flexible and designed to influence the whole personality, to deal with a failure not just of education but also of social adaptation and competence. It stimulated activity on the man's own part so that literacy was seen to be a purposeful activity relevant to his own life as a soldier and citizen.

The catalyst in the training process was the special relationship between instructor and student—a relationship that provided stability and authority without repression.

The whole ethos of the school was an active testimony to the following statement in the *Newsom Report* regarding the significant influence of the social and physical environment: "Since these are susceptible to modification they may well prove educationally more important" (Ministry of Education, 1963). The results of such modification in terms of academic success and also in personality development are examined and discussed at length in the chapters that follow. It may well be, however, that the work and success of the SPE in this field indicates a vital need for research into what is and what is not feasible in education training in these days of harsh economic reality and ever-escalating costs.

---

*Vacation camps at a number of seaside resorts in England and Wales.

4 Environmental Factors and Reading Achievement

We aren't no thin red 'eroes, an' we aren't no blackguards too.
But single men in barricks, most remarkable like you.

RUDYARD KIPLING

The *Plowden Report* (Ministry of Education, 1967) states "A child is most at risk when the influence of home and school run counter to each other." This chapter examines these influences as they have affected the lives of educationally backward soldiers, and seeks to establish which factors were significant in inhibiting the development of their full intellectual potential.

Because of the importance of environmental factors in cognitive development and in the full development of language, it seemed relevant to examine any notable differences in socio-cultural experiences within this superficially homogeneous group and to relate them to linguistic performance. On the basis of reading achievement on the Holborn Reading Scale, the sample population was divided into three groups: poor readers, mediocre readers, and good readers. The aim of this threefold classification was to identify the two groups of men at each end of the reading-ability continuum, and also those who possessed some mechanical fluency but were not able to read in really meaningful terms with effective transfer to other learning.

The three groups were classified according to the following criteria:

Poor readers (N = 140)	A reading age of 9 years or less, coinciding with Burt's definition of the level of semi-illiteracy
Mediocre readers (N = 520)	A reading age of more than 9 years but not greater than 12 years
Good readers (N = 100)	A reading age of more than 12 years

THE INSTRUMENT OF SOCIOLOGICAL INQUIRY

Since the pioneering work of men like Burt and Schonell, it has been recognized that backwardness in educational attainment is frequently associated with differences in personality created by physical and environmental circumstances. Schonell (1942) writes: "Recent research and records from class teaching indicate, however, that its explanation (i.e. backwardness) is more likely to be found in a study of the pupil's entire personality!"

Such a study had long been accepted at the School of Preliminary Education as a particularly vital factor in educational therapy, and the questionnaire shown in Appendix B was designed to enable the instructor to set down relevant information with the minimum inconvenience. The bulk of the information was obtained during individual interviews in the first few days of the course, since it was only possible to sensitively evaluate each man's particular difficulties, and determine how these could best be alleviated, when all the contributory factors had been examined. However, as the rapport between instructor and the student increased, further information would be added as gaps in background knowledge were filled.

The questionnaire shown is a copy of one that was completed for a student in the sample population. It illustrates the detailed information the instructor obtained in order to understand the problems associated with each individual's backwardness and to serve as a base from which to begin the assault upon his actual difficulties. Rarely was there any reluctance on the part of the student to divulge the information. In fact, most of the men seemed greatly relieved to have had the opportunity of pouring out the most intimate facts concerning their lives to someone who they felt was interested and sympathetic. This in itself indicates the lack of adequate adult relationships in the lives of most of them.

HOME AREAS

The student population was heterogeneous, comprising English, Scots, Welsh, Irish, and a small number of immigrants (mostly West Indians). Table 4.1 shows the home areas of the three reading groups based on natural geographical divisions, which contain at least one major recruiting office. The table also shows the percentage distribution by home area for the total sample.

These figures in themselves are not significant since they represented only that part of the population that volunteered for military service, but they do indicate the school's nationwide "catchment area." Certain areas had a high percentage of recruits who were poor readers (Southampton, 38.1 percent; Birmingham and Mid-Wales, 25.9 percent; Bristol, South Wales, and the South West, 23.1 percent). This may indicate poorer employment prospects for semi-illiterate male adults in these particular areas, thus making Army life appear more attractive. Of those recruited from Birmingham and Mid-Wales, some 95 percent were actually from the Birmingham district. The high incidence of poor readers in this group would appear to confirm the findings of the Pringle and Bossio Survey (1958) in which it was found that the proportion of slow children from that area was higher, that of bright children lower, than among school children generally nationwide. The survey was particularly concerned about the extent of backwardness in language development and the fact that backwardness in reading comprehension was at least twice as great as in the normal school population. Since the average age of the total sample population was 18 years 9 months, these soldiers were in primary school at the time of the Pringle and Bossio Survey, and their low level of attainment on enlistment bears out the findings and fears of the report.

Breakdown into Urban and Rural

Table 4.1 also shows the distribution between reading groups of men with rural and urban backgrounds. Of the total, 76.9 percent come from urban backgrounds as opposed to 23.1 percent from rural. It is interesting that, while the proportions of poor readers from the two backgrounds differ considerably (26.9 percent rural and 15.9 percent urban), the differences between the reading groups with regard to the different backgrounds are statistically highly significant ($P < 0.01$). Thus, in this particular sample, there appears to be a close association between a rural upbringing and poor reading ability.

TABLE 4.1. Home Area Distribution

	POOR READERS (N=140)	MEDIOCRE READERS (N=520)	GOOD READERS (N=100)	TOTAL (N=760)
GEOGRAPHICAL DIVISIONS				
Birmingham and Mid Wales	21	53	7	81 (10.7%)
Bristol, S. Wales, and S. West	15	45	5	65 (8.6%)
Derby, Notts, and Lincs	9	29	9	47 (6.1%)
Scotland	13	57	14	84 (11.1%)
Liverpool, S. Lancs, Cheshire, and N. Wales	22	70	20	112 (14.9%)
London and East Anglia	21	73	16	110 (14.5%)
Yorkshire	13	88	13	114 (15.0%)
Newcastle, Durham, and Cumberland	5	26	5	36 (4.7%)
Southampton and South	8	10	3	21 (2.8%)
Ireland	8	29	4	41 (5.4%)
Overseas	5	40	4	49 (6.5%)
URBAN / RURAL DIVISION				
Urban	93	416	76	585
Rural	47	104	24	175

TABLE 4.2. Changes in Home Area

	P (N=140)	M (N=520)	G (N=100)
Mean number of changes	2.8	2.6	2.7
Number with no change	36	12	18

Note: Mean number of changes per total sample population = 2.6.

Changes of Home Area

Changes of home area do not appear to have been a significant factor affecting the level of attainment since the mean number of changes for the total sample is only 2.6. Table 4.2 shows that while poor readers have the highest mean number of changes with 2.8, they also contain by far the highest percentage of those with no change. Unexpectedly the differences in mean number of changes for all reading groups are so small as to be insignificant. The small number of changes generally was lower than anticipated, since one would expect to associate frequent changes of home, and consequently of school, with poor overall attainment.

SOCIO-ECONOMIC STATUS OF THE FAMILY

Occupation of Father

The distribution of fathers' occupations among the reading groups is shown in Table 4.3. It can be seen that 69.2 percent of the fathers are manual workers and 59 percent of those are in the unskilled category. Although all occupational grades are represented in each reading group, the high percentage of fathers concentrated in the manual grades is unmistakable. Sample G has, as expected, the lowest percentage (59) in this category and the highest percentage for the professional grade. Taking into consideration the relatively high number of fathers deceased (12.1 percent), those who are unemployed or permanent invalids, and those employed in manual labor, 85.3 percent of the students come from homes that have a low economic level.

This study therefore confirms the findings of Morris (1966) in the Kent survey that showed a close association between poor reading ability and the fathers' occupations. Also confirmed were the findings of Fraser (1959) who stated "although there is a close relationship between the father's occupation and the IQ of the child, there is a significantly closer relationship between the father's occupation and the child's school success."

Occupation of Mother

> The hand that rocks the cradle is the most potent force—Plowden Report. (Ministry of Education, 1967)

In my investigation mothers of students have been classified into four groups: (1) those who are housewives only; (2) those with a part-

TABLE 4.3. Occupation of Father

OCCUPATION	P (N=140)	M (N=520)	G (N=100)	TOTAL (N=760)
Professional	3	18	5	26 (3.4%)
Higher Clerical	2	6	2	10 (1.3%)
Lower Clerical	2	2	3	7 (0.9%)
Retail	3	11	4	18 (2.4%)
Self-Employed	9	5	4	18 (2.4%)
Manual: Skilled	47	140	29	216 (28.4%)
Unskilled	47	233	30	310 (40.8%)
Unemployed	4	18	2	24 (3.2%)
Permanent Invalid	1	—	5	6 (0.8%)
Deceased	14	68	10	92 (12.1%)
TOTAL	132	501	94	727
Reared in Orphanage/ Whereabouts Unknown	8	19	6	33 (4.3%)

TABLE 4.4. Employment and Availability of Mother During Formative Years

	P	M	G	TOTAL
EMPLOYMENT				
Housewife only	26	181	30	237 (32.6%)
Part-time	38	161	16	215 (29.6%)
Full-time	58	125	39	222 (30.5%)
Deceased	11	33	9	53 (9.3%)
TOTAL	133	500	94	727
AVAILABILITY				
Available	26	181	30	237 (31.2%)
Not available	114	339	70	523 (68.8%)
TOTAL	140	520	100	760

time job outside the home; (3) those with a full-time job outside the home; (4) those who are deceased. The classification was for the period during the soldiers' formative preschool and school years rather than at the time of the SPE course, although this distinction would have had little effect upon the findings.

The most striking factor of the figures shown in Table 4.4 is the very low percentage (32.6 percent) of mothers who, during these men's formative years, were housewives only. While there is little difference between the percentage in samples M and G, that of sample P is significantly lower at only 18.6 percent. The difference between the groups of readers compared with the availability and nonavailability of mothers during the formative years is statistically highly significant ($P < 0.01$) (see Table 4.4). The figures make an interesting comparison with those obtained by Morris (1966) in the Kent Survey; he found that approximately 68 percent and 51 percent of mothers in samples G and P, respectively, were housewives only. This considerable difference is explained to some extent by the fact that, in the Kent Survey, the children were drawn from much broader economic levels of the population. Whereas 69.2 percent of the fathers of my sample population belong to the manual occupational grades, only 36.5 percent of the Kent children had fathers in these categories. The percentage of soldiers from homes with a low economic level is, therefore, almost twice that in the Kent Survey. My study gives support to the results of Wiseman's (1968) factor analysis that shows that "poor educational attainment with low average scores, low percentage of bright children and high percentage of backward children are found in association with a low economic level."

However, as a result of some six years' experience with these soldiers' educational and emotional problems, I believe that the high proportion of mothers with either part- or full-time employment has a much deeper significance. The majority of these mothers had taken some form of employment, predominantly unskilled manual, because of sheer economic necessity; yet at the same time they have been burdened with the responsibility of coping with families considerably larger than the national average. In such circumstances it seems that the efficiency of the mother, which Burt (1937) describes as being "the one factor which showed the closest correlation to the child's school progress," must be impaired. The mother comes home "too tired," and thus there is insufficient direction in the home, a lack of stimulation and socialization, and a consequent impoverishment of language.

The comments of students and the letters from students' homes indicate that most of these mothers were over-burdened by domestic worries; in some cases this led to an almost complete abdication of parental responsibility. Against this must be set the findings of Fraser (1959) that in only 2 out of 107 cases involving working mothers was there an adverse comment on the interview form about care of the home. Also there is the very relevant fact that, if these mothers had not undertaken some type of employment, the soldiers would in many cases have suffered even greater social and economic deprivation.

The findings from this study are, therefore, that a higher than average proportion of working mothers is to be found among this population drawn from a low economic level and that this proportion is particularly high among those with severe reading difficulties.

OTHER FACTORS IN THE FAMILY

Size of Family

The mean number of children per family in the total sample is 5.5. The mean number by each reading ability group is poor readers, 6.1; mediocre readers, 5.4; and good readers, 4.8. The figures are considerably higher than the national average of 2.2 and, as would be expected, increase as the level of reading ability decreases.

A distribution of family size for each reading group is shown in Table 4.5. While 28 (3.7 percent) of the sample are only children, and 42.9

TABLE 4.5. Distribution of Family Size

NUMBER OF SIBLINGS PER FAMILY	NUMBERS OF FAMILIES			
	P (N=140)	M (N=520)	G (N=100)	TOTAL (N=760)
1	2	14	12	28 (3.7%)
2	7	46	11	64 (8.4%)
3	24	58	18	100 (13.2%)
4	18	86	15	119 (15.7%)
5	21	104	12	137 (17.9%)
6	15	66	8	89 (11.7%)
7	15	49	5	69 (9.1%)
8	12	34	6	52 (6.8%)
9	4	24	4	32 (4.2%)
10	7	12	2	21 (2.8%)
11	3	11	4	18 (2.4%)
12	6	5	1	12 (1.6%)
13	1	6	—	7 (0.9%)
14	4	2	1	7 (0.9%)
15	—	—	—	—
16	1	1	—	2 (0.3%)
17	—	2	1	3 (0.4%)

percent of these are good readers, there are 70 families (9.7 percent) with 10 or more children. The figures confirm the findings of the *Crowther Report* (Ministry of Education, 1960) that the less skilled the occupational group, the larger is the size of the family. Since, with a few exceptions, these men are of below-average ability, my study also supports the findings of Nisbet (1953) that IQ is negatively correlated with size of family.

Reliable figures on birth order could not be obtained as many of these men are unsure of the ages of their brothers and sisters. In those cases where exact ages of all siblings were known (i.e., some 76 percent) 78 percent of the soldiers were the last born. However, no conclusions may be drawn from this in the absence of any information or records concerning the educational standard of the other siblings.

Broken Homes and Stability of Home Circumstances

For the purposes of this study broken homes were defined as those where there had been a death of one or both parents, a divorce, or a separation, or where there were no known parents. The distribution of broken homes between the reading groups is shown in Table 4.6.

TABLE 4.6. Homes with Unstable Circumstances

HOME SITUATION	P	M	G	TOTAL
BROKEN HOMES				
Father deceased	20	61	9	90
Mother deceased	11	33	7	51
Both parents deceased	—	—	2	2
Divorced/separated	19	57	13	89
Parents unknown	3	3		6
Reared in orphanage	4	17	6	27
TOTAL	57 (40.7%)	171 (33.9%)	37 (37%)	265 (34.9%)
DIFFICULT HOMES				
Frequent quarrels	34	107	28	169 (22.2%)
Frequent quarrels with violence	17	51	13	81 (10.7%)
TOTAL	51	158	41	250 (32.9%)
Students worried by quarrelsome situation	19	51	19	89 (35.6%)

The proportion of broken homes is greatest among the poor readers (40.7 percent), but the differences between groups are not statistically significant, and all the figures are very high in comparison with those found in other studies. Morris (1966) in the Kent Survey found 24.6 percent from broken homes, while Mannheim and Wilkins (1955) found that only 14 percent of the young adolescent population fell into this category compared with 22 percent of those who were in borstal training.*

Taking into account all the factors, 26.3 percent of the men in the total sample were deprived of paternal influence (Morris finds only 4 percent), and I found this to be an important factor in their attitude to Army life and the SPE course in particular. My experience and investigation led me to conclude that most of these men, including those whose fathers are still alive, have missed the security, stability, and authority of an adequate relationship with a male adult. The need they have felt for this is apparent in the way in which they readily place the instructor officer at SPE in the role of Father Confessor. In addition, Army life is in many respects tailor-made to compensate for these deficiencies since the men are absolved from involvement in the major decisions of daily life, which is governed by rules and regulations not subject to the fluctuations of unstable home conditions.

A deprivation of paternal care, love, and authority is not the only adverse circumstance in many of these men's lives. Table 4.6 also shows the distribution of homes where frequent serious quarrels have disrupted interpersonal relations.

Nearly one-third of the students (32.9 percent) have home backgrounds where frequent quarrels have been a feature of family life; 10.7 percent have lived in conditions where the quarrels were actually accompanied by physical violence. In many instances a man has suffered both from the loss of a parent and from very unstable family relationships. Also from broken homes were 52.6 percent of those whose homes were the scene of frequent serious quarrels and 38.3 percent of those in whose homes the quarrels were accompanied by violence. In total, therefore, 51.9 percent of the sample have home circumstances that may be expected to have adversely affected their attitudes. The differences between the distribution of these in the reading groups is not statistically significant.

That those men have been considerably affected by their unfortun-

*A modified form of prison treatment for persons aged 16–21 years.

ate experiences is evidenced by the number (35.6 percent) who confess to having been seriously worried or upset by them, and also by their frequent references to them in personal interviews. One student recalls:

> He [his father] never done a stroke in the home, nothing except getting drunk every night when he came home and knocked the old lady about and us kids as well if we was about. He run off in the end with a big blond bird from the pub when I was 9 and we all said, "Thank God."

Another who had considerable difficulty in reading, and even in writing his own name, required psychiatric treatment for acute anxiety neurosis as a result of his father's efforts at educating him: "He sat me at the table with a book and if I made a mistake he belted me one—sometimes with a leather strap, sometimes with the butt of his shotgun and sometimes he ONLY used his fists!"

Yet another stated: "I ain't never seen her [his mother] but my dad says she's a right cow playing about with anyone she fancies."

Having been required to investigate the deep-seated emotional problems that are the aftermath of such adverse environmental conditions, I find it difficult to understand how Warburton (1968) could ask: "Why should a lack of love and affection inhibit ability in reading?" or that Freeman and Showell (1953) should state: "It seems unlikely that the family influence is as important as our literature suggests." It is surely the very quality of the actual family relationships that is so important and that was rightly stressed in the *Crowther Report* (Ministry of Education, 1960). I certainly believe that the effectiveness of the parents as models, the values they offer, and their attitudes to education are very important factors. Lack of parental encouragement had depressed these men's ability to express themselves and to utilize efficiently whatever intellectual aptitudes they may have. A student stated: "Why should I bother about them [his parents and family] or go home at weekends when all they do is taken the mickey out of me because I can't read too good!"

Since there is no statistical significance between the distribution of difficult home circumstances in the reading groups in Table 4.6, reading disability cannot be attributed to the adverse effects of these home circumstances alone. However, the findings of this study do indicate that an abnormal home background is a factor closely associated with general educational backwardness in men from lower class backgrounds.

CULTURAL STANDARDS IN THE HOME

Availability of Adult Reading Books

Obtaining reasonably accurate figures concerning the availability of adult reading books in the home presented some difficulty, since an adult "book" to many of these men, and apparently to many of their fathers, was frequently regarded as one that consisted mainly of a series of photographs of young women in a state of semi or total nudity. An analysis of the information obtained is shown at Table 4.7, but it may well be that even the high percentage (38.3 percent) of men from homes with no books available actually underestimates the true facts.

The figures may at first sight appear to contradict expectations since the percentage of poor readers from homes with many books (10 percent) is five times that of the good readers (2 percent). Since, also, there are fewer poor readers (30 percent) than good readers (36 percent) from homes with no books, the poor readers do not appear to have been at a disadvantage regarding the availability of reading material in the home. There are, however, two important factors that have contributed to this apparent discrepancy. The first is that the 14 poor readers from homes with many books were all men of average or above average intelligence from small families but who were suffering from some spe-

TABLE 4.7. Availability of Reading Material in the Home

READING MATERIAL	P (N=140)	M (N=520)	G (N=100)	TOTAL (N=760)
BOOKS				
Homes with many	14	58	2	74 (9.7%)
Homes with only a few	84	249	62	395 (52%)
Homes with none	42	213	36	291 (38.3%)
NEWSPAPERS				
Taken regularly	99	477	89	665 (87.5%)
Taken occasionally	5	36	9	50 (6.6%)
None available	36	7	2	45 (5.9%)

cific disability: 10 were suffering from developmental dyslexia* and associated emotional disorders; two were in serious need of glasses; and the remaining two suffered from acute emotional stress as a result of broken homes. The second factor is that the good readers, with adequate mechanical fluency and comprehension, understood the concept of an "adult" book far more readily than did some of the men with subnormal intelligence in the poor reading group. For these reasons I believe that the figure for the group of homes with no books available may reflect the facts more accurately than the figure for the poor readers. However, it cannot be inferred from this study that a plentiful supply of books at home is related to the reading skills of these backward men.

Availability of Daily Newspapers in the Home

Table 4.7 also shows a comparison of the three reading groups in relation to the availability of daily newspapers as reading material in the home and reveals marked differences in favor of the good readers. Eighty-nine percent of them had regular access to daily newspapers, and only 2 percent were from homes where no newspapers were available. In contrast, 70.7 percent of the poor readers were able to see a daily newspaper, and 25.7 percent had no access to one. It was not possible to obtain any reliable information about the actual newspapers that were available since many men could not recall which newspapers had actually been taken at home. The value of chi-square shows the relationship between the availability of newspapers in the home and the three reading groups to be highly significant ($P < 0.001$).

Membership in Public Libraries

It was not possible to obtain any accurate records of parents' membership in the public library service and to examine whether the example set had been followed by the children regardless of reading ability. The figures for student membership of public libraries are shown in Table 4.8.

A total of 24.1 percent of the men had at some time regularly used the public library service, which would appear to reflect initial parental

---

**Developmental dyslexia* is defined by the World Federation of Neurologists as a disorder manifested by difficulty in learning to read despite conventional instruction, adequate intelligence, and socio-cultural opportunity. It is dependent upon fundamental cognitive disabilities that are frequently of constitutional origin.

TABLE 4.8. Students' Public Library Membership and Purchase of Reading Materials

	P (N=140)	M (N=520)	G (N=100)	TOTAL (N=760)
PUBLIC LIBRARY				
Member	51	90	42	183 (24.1%)
Nonmember	89	430	58	577 (75.9%)
READING MATERIAL PURCHASED				
Comics	11	164	9	184 (24.2%)
War story comics	22	9	14	45 (5.9%)
Magazines	54	227	54	335 (44.1%)
None	53	120	23	196 (25.8%)

encouragement followed by their own lack of enthusiasm. The most interesting feature is the very small percentage (17.3 percent) of mediocre readers who belonged to the library service compared with 36.4 percent of the poor readers and 42 percent of the good readers. The group of good readers would be expected to show the most interest in reading as a leisure activity, but it may well be that the high percentage of poor readers shows that many really felt their disability and were striving to improve themselves—this applies particularly to those of average and above-average intelligence. The mediocre readers, on the other hand, may well have reached a stage of mechanical fluency that they felt was sufficient to meet their everyday needs but was insufficient to spur them to use books either for pleasure or for transfer to other learning. The value of chi-square obtained for the relationship between reading groups and membership of the public library service is highly significant ($P < 0.001$). Thus, all that may be concluded from the present study is that those men with a superior reading ability showed the greatest interest in reading as an enjoyable leisure activity.

Reading Material Purchased Regularly

The three reading groups were also compared in respect to the type of reading material that they purchased regularly for themselves. It is readily seen from Table 4.8 that no real adult "books" were mentioned in their answers.

Of the sample 25.8 percent admitted that they never purchased any type of reading material whatsoever, and it is not surprising that the difference between the good readers (23 percent) and poor readers (37.9 percent) is statistically significant in this respect.

At first sight it is surprising that 9 percent of good readers purchased comics compared with only 7.8 percent of poor readers. I investigated this in some detail and the difference arises from the varying types of comics that are available. Whereas the poor readers purchased only the comics that may be fully comprehended by purely pictorial means (e.g., *Beano* and *TV Comic*), the good readers purchased the more sophisticated variety that feature stories (e.g., *Valiant*). Nearly one-third (31.5 percent) of the mediocre readers bought comics regularly, and 61 percent of these were of a pictorial nature. The mediocre reading group had little enthusiasm for war story comics, so greatly favored almost equally by the poor and good readers.

The answers given regarding the purchase of magazines required considerable analysis, and again there was a marked difference in type of material chosen by the poor and good readers. Whereas 85 percent of the latter purchased magazines of a specialist nature (*Hobbies, Motor-Cycle*), 94.4 percent of the poor readers concentrated their expenditure on the type designed to stimulate erotic feelings. The value of chi-square obtained for the relationship between the reading groups and the type of reading material purchased is highly significant ($P < 0.001$). Thus, this study finds that reading ability is a significant factor with regard to the cultural level of material likely to be purchased regularly. If the figures of reading within homes are some indication of cultural levels, they also show how the low standards prevailing in the majority of cases have adversely affected the men's own standards and levels of interest.

SCHOOL CONDITIONS AND ATTITUDE TO SCHOOLING

Size of Classes

In the first diagnostic interviews the students were questioned closely about the size of classes at both primary and secondary school levels. While many could not remember the exact numbers in the classes, they did recall the approximate size (e.g., they knew whether the figure was nearer 30 than 40). The figures obtained indicate that there was no significant difference between any of the reading groups (see Table 4.9).

TABLE 4.9. Approximate Size of Classes

	CLASS SIZE		
SCHOOL LEVEL	P	M	G
Primary	40	38	40
Secondary	25	28	26

TABLE 4.10. Attitudes Toward School

ATTITUDE	P (N = 140)	M (N = 520)	G (N = 100)	TOTAL (N = 760)
Actively disliked school	41	78	15	134 (17.6%)
Positively liked school	58	309	64	431 (56.7%)
Totally indifferent	41	133	21	195 (25.7%)

When Kemp (1955) and Warburton (1968) studied less restricted ability groups, they found no correlation between class size and educational attainment. The figures obtained within this special group confirm this.

Number of Changes of School

No significant differences were found between the reading ability groups regarding the number of schools actually attended. Discounting the change from primary to secondary level, the mean number of changes for the whole population was found to be 2.3. The mean figures for the three groups do not differ significantly from this and are as follows: poor readers, 2.2; mediocre readers, 2.3; and good readers, 2.1.

Thus this investigation cannot conclude that the number of changes of school is a factor in relation to reading ability.

Attitude Toward School

Although 56.7 percent of the sample stated that they had positively liked school, 17.6 percent had actively disliked it (see Table 4.10). Significant differences are found between the poor readers and the mediocre and good readers. The percentage of poor readers who actively disliked school is nearly twice that of the mediocre and good groups. Sixty-four percent of good readers and 59.4 percent of the mediocre groups positively liked school compared with approximately 41.4 percent of the poor readers. This is not unexpected, however, since reading is one of the most important developmental tasks, and failure in reading is likely to affect attitudes and interpersonal relations. Conversely, it may well be that the failure to read has arisen from inefficient teaching and/or failure of the school organization. Are we, as Riesman (1950) suggests, probing too much in the out of school environment for causes for the poor performances of the underprivileged and paying too little attention to the faults of the schools? Are these men who so disliked school the victims of nonperceptive teachers or of the inability of some teachers and schools to make effective personal contact?

This study does not provide definitive answers to these questions. The indications are, however, that teacher attitudes and perceptions did play a not unimportant role in creating some of the antipathy that many of these men felt toward education. The study does show that those with superior reading ability are likely to have a more positive attitude toward school and the learning process.

Attitudes Toward Teachers and Other Children

Questions and discussion concerning their attitudes toward teachers tended to produce a more emotional response from these men than did the most intimate probing of all other environmental circumstances. There was a strong and conscious feeling among the majority that they had been permanently "labeled"; that they were backward and that nothing could be done about it. In many cases it is tragically obvious that no properly organized attempt had been made to do anything about it.

A total of 22.4 percent felt quite definitely that they had been picked on by their teacher because of their disability in reading. One student recalled:

> He [the teacher] said I was too stupid and thick to do anything else so I just drawed and played with plasticine when the others had books or writing. 'Course I was right at the back of the class out of his way and so I never done nothing at all. He never bothered so long as I wasn't no trouble.

It is perhaps worth recording that this man actually had an IQ of 112. A natural left hander, he had been forced by a teacher to change handedness, and in consequence he was a forced cross-lateral. His writing was a mass of reversals and reoriented symbols. His antipathy toward teachers is therefore hardly surprising.

A total of 170 men felt that they had been picked on constantly by their teachers. The distribution between reading groups is as follows: poor readers, 30; mediocre readers, 119; and good readers, 21. The interesting feature of these figures is that the percentage of men holding this view is practically equal in each of the groups. The feeling, therefore, is not confined to those men with the greatest disability in reading but is spread evenly throughout the whole sample; this study thus lends support to Castle's (1954) findings that in a normal classroom the more difficult and educationally retarded tend to receive less sympathetic treatment from their teachers.

In marked contrast to their attitudes and feelings toward teachers, very few of these men appear to have suffered any difficulty in interpersonal relations with other children during their own childhood. Only 4.6 percent (37 men) of the total sample suggested that they had been picked on by other children while at school. The division of these men among the reading groups is interesting since, quite contrary to my expectations, only 5 percent of poor readers felt they had been picked on, compared with 9 percent of the good readers. Somewhat surprisingly, therefore, this study does not support the research of Hargreaves (1967) who at Lumley School found that the unfortunate attitudes of some teachers toward the less able pupils were also reflected in the attitudes of the more able children.

Absence from School Through Illness

Warburton (1968) finds good attainment to be very closely associated with a high attendance record. It might be expected, therefore, that there would be a significant difference in the attendance records between the poor and good readers in this sample population. It was not possible to obtain detailed and accurate school-attendance records for these men. To simplify the problem for them, they were asked at interviews whether or not they had had one or more periods of absence of more than 6 weeks because of illness. It was considered that this period of time (half a term) constituted a significant break in the educational process. As shown in Table 4.11, 17.6 percent were found to have had at least one period of absence for this time. Only 8 percent of good readers had suffered from a long absence compared with 20 percent of the mediocre readers and 15.7 percent of the poor readers. Since the difference between the good readers and the other two groups is statistically significant, this study appears to confirm Warburton's conclu-

TABLE 4.11. School Absence Due to Illness

	P (N=140)	M (N=520)	G (N=100)	TOTAL (N=760)
Absence of more than 6 weeks	22	104	8	134 (17.6%)
No long absence	118	416	92	626 (82.4%)

TABLE 4.12. Total Number of Truants and Nontruants

	P (N=140)	M (N=520)	G (N=100)	TOTAL (N=760)
Truants	31	120	17	168
Nontruants	109	400	83	592

sions that lack of attainment in reading is associated with a poor attendance record.

Absence from School Through Truancy

The Extent of Truancy

Truancy is an offence against the law, but, as Tyerman (1958) points out, it is a sin of omission rather than commission. Nevertheless, it appeared that truancy would be an important aspect of this investigation, since studies show that a considerable number of other delinquencies stem from it. It also appeared particularly relevant because studies indicate that the main causes of truancy seem to be poor home conditions, inferior ability, and intellectual and social failure at school with consequent feelings of unhappiness, inferiority, and frustration.

The actual extent of truancy in the schools' population is unknown since the DES and LEAs do not make public the number of prosecutions or interviews conducted by attendance committees for truancy or for withholding a child from school. For the purposes of this study truancy was classified as habitual nonattendance for at least one full day per week during the secondary stage of education, since this experience was sufficiently recent for the subjects to recall with some accuracy. Table 4.12 shows the extent of truancy within the sample population.

The figures indicate that 22.1 percent of the sample indulged in habitual truancy. The percentages of poor readers and mediocre readers who thus absented themselves from school for 20 percent of the school year are 22.1 percent and 23.1 percent as compared with only 17 percent for the group of good readers. The value of chi-square shows the difference between the groups to be significant ($P < 0.50$). Besides the 168 men comprising this hardened group of absentees, an additional 305 men (40.1 percent of the sample) confessed to playing truant on a somewhat irregular basis. In this instance the difference between the reading groups was highly significant, there being only 15 percent of good readers compared with 57.1 percent of poor readers and 40.4 percent of mediocre readers. Thus, in this sample we find a total of 62.2 percent (474 men) who are deliberately opting out of the educational system either with or without collusion at home. Twenty-seven actually stated that they were often kept at home to look after younger brothers and sisters while their mothers went to work. A nonreader, aged 43, one of a family of nine children and now himself married with five children, stated on interview:

> I never 'ad no school after I was 9. I 'ad to stay at 'ome and do all the old woman's jobs whilst she went down the factory. I done all the washing, all the cleaning like a proper scivvy. Then at nights I 'ad to put them all to bed while she went down to the bleeding pub. I got a kid sitting GCE next year so 'ow do I feel when she says she can't understand one of them Shakespeare books. Understand it! I can't even bleeding read it!

The extent of truancy in this sample thus presents a very sobering picture. The success of 62.3 percent of this sample in avoiding school has serious implications. Not only does this again focus attention on the type of curriculum that is reinforcing failure and creating unhappiness at school, but it may well have unfortunate repercussions in that, having thus successfully avoided school, those concerned may be led to believe that they can just as easily succeed with other forms of delinquency and a vicious circle begins.

Distribution of Truants in Urban and Rural Areas

The truants in the three reading groups were compared in respect to urban or rural background. The distribution is shown in Table 4.13, and the value of chi-square obtained for the relationship between the groups is highly significant ($P < 0.001$).

The most interesting aspect of these figures is the surprisingly

TABLE 4.13. Distribution of Truants by Urban and Rural Backgrounds

	P	M	G	TOTAL
Urban	29	27	14	70
Rural	2	93	3	98
TOTAL	31	120	17	168

TABLE 4.14. Number of Truants and Nontruants from Broken Homes

	P	M	G	TOTAL
Truants	14	53	14	81
Nontruants	43	118	23	184
TOTAL	57	171	37	265

greater incidence of habitual truancy in the rural areas. Of the total numbers living in urban areas, only 11.9 percent were hardened offenders compared with 56 percent of those who lived in rural districts, but I could not establish any reason for this other than that the country boys appeared to be more bored with the school curriculum than were their urban counterparts. It is possible that, in the years when these men were at school, the smaller rural schools had a more uninteresting and less enlightened curriculum than is now the case. It is also more difficult to check on attendance in rural areas where homes are widely dispersed. The main attractions seemed to be going off in pursuit of country sports such as fishing and poaching in addition to "helping down the farm."

The figures relating to the distribution of truants from urban areas between the poor and good reading groups differ significantly, however. In this respect, this study finds a relationship between reading failure and truancy, and thus lends support to the findings of Tyerman (1958) that truancy is an escape from this unacceptable situation.

Broken Homes and Truancy

The distribution of truants and nontruants from broken homes was compared by reading groups (see Table 4.14), and the differences were found to be statistically significant ($P < 0.50$). Of the total of 168 truants, 48.2 percent came from broken homes indicating a high truancy risk among pupils from this type of environment.

This study thus lends support to Tyerman's (1958) findings that apparently one-third of the truants were not living with both parents and that in three-fourths of the homes studied there was no real family feeling.

Other Environmental Factors and Truancy

Appendix C shows the distribution by reading groups for other environmental factors and truancy.

EMPLOYMENT

Preenlistment Occupation

On average these men had some 2–3 years' experience working in a civilian capacity before enlistment. An analysis of their first civilian occupations is shown in Table 4.15. This data closely mirror the pattern of the fathers' occupations in Table 4.3 with the majority (81.3 percent) entering the manual grades. Those entering skilled manual occupations (i.e., apprenticeships) and the lower clerical grades come almost entirely from among the most able readers, clearly indicating that the level of employment obtained upon leaving school is related to reading ability.

The determinants in the choice of first civilian occupations of the full sample were

Liked the idea	48.8 percent
Directed	28.3 percent
Only job available	22.9 percent

There was a marked bias in favor of the most able readers, since only 17 percent of this group were required to accept the only job available compared with 40.7 percent of the poor readers. Approximately 90 percent of those "directed" (by tradition or other influences) toward particular employment had been told, "It would be a good thing for you."

Since most of these men attended SPE within 2 or 3 weeks of enlistment, their civilian employment should have been fresh in their memories, but even so many found it difficult to remember exactly how many and what particular jobs they had held. In some cases this was because they had held as many as 15 different jobs in less than 3 years. Thus it was difficult to obtain accurate information on this aspect of their employment records, and the mean number of job changes (4.4

for the sample group) probably errs somewhat on the low side. The reasons given for changes of employment were usually "to better myself" or "more money and better conditions." That these aims had seldom been achieved and that at least 38 percent had been dismissed from at least one job served to increase their sense of failure and emphasize to them the way in which educational backwardness restricts an applicant to unskilled work or casual labor.

Only 66 men (8.7 percent) remained in their original employment until enlistment. Of this group, 56 men (84.9 percent) were employed in the mining industry and had taken this employment because of family tradition. These men had only left to join the Army because of the closing of coal mines.

Table 4.16 compares the mean number of changes of employment between those from stable and adverse home environments. The mean number of changes for the whole sample is 4.4. In the case of those from broken homes, it appears that the instability that had been a feature of their daily lives had been carried forward into their employment records. Besides, fewer of these men in each of the three reading-ability groups had only one civilian job before enlistment.

The findings of Trenaman (1952) and Tyerman (1958) that truants often have a very poor employment record are borne out by this study. Table 4.16 also shows the number of job changes of truants and nontruants. The interesting aspect of these figures is that the mean number of changes of employment for truant poor and good readers is 6.1, considerably higher than the comparable figures of 4.3 and 3.4 for nontruants and also higher than the mean of 4.4 for the whole sample. In this case the evidence shows that the unhappiness, frustration, and anxiety associated with truancy appears to predispose these men to instability in their employment.

In the short duration of their civilian employment, reading ability had not had time to show any notable correlation with remuneration. In fact, the opposite appears to be the case, since the mean weekly salaries for the groups (to the nearest pound) were poor readers, £15; mediocre readers, £14; and good readers, £11. These figures are somewhat misleading, however, since the majority of men in the poor and mediocre groups were employed in unskilled manual jobs that have no pay structure geared to training and promotion and pay comparatively well initially. The good readers either serving apprenticeships or starting in the lower clerical grades were thus in occupations that would bear fruit financially in later years. It appears from this study then that the employment prospects of school leavers are closely associated with educational attainment.

TABLE 4.15. Classification of First Civilian Occupation

TYPE OF OCCUPATION	NUMBER=760	PERCENTAGE
MANUAL		
Skilled	99	13.0%
Unskilled	519	68.3%
RETAIL	129	17.0%
CLERICAL		
Higher	—	
Lower	12	1.6%
SELF-EMPLOYED	1	0.1%

TABLE 4.16. Analysis of Changes of Employment by Home Stability and Truancy

	P (N=140)	M (N=520)	G (N=100)
BROKEN HOMES			
Mean number of changes	5.2	4.1	4.9
Number of men with one change	6	19	4
NONBROKEN HOMES			
Mean number of changes	4.4	4.5	3.2
Number of men with one change	9	21	6
TRUANTS			
Mean number of changes	6.1	5.2	6.1
Number of men with one change	1	14	2
NONTRUANTS			
Mean number of changes	4.3	4.2	3.4
Number of men with one change	14	26	8

TABLE 4.17. Analysis of Reasons for Enlistment

REASON	P (N=140)	M (N=520)	G (N=100)	TOTAL (N=760)
To learn a trade	83 (59.3%)	322 (61.9%)	67 (67.0%)	472 (62.1%)
To become better educated	16 (11.4%)	3 (0.6%)	3 (3.0%)	22 (2.9%)
To have security	15 (10.7%)	71 (13.7%)	8 (8.0%)	94 (12.4%)

Present Aspirations

The trend in employment at the present is shifting strongly in favor of highly trained people working in professional and technical occupations, with a decrease in the number of manual and unskilled jobs. The civilian experience of these men had probably made them well aware that educational backwardness is a serious occupational handicap; this is shown in Table 4.17, an analysis of their reasons for enlistment.

A majority of men in all groups desired an education that involved acquiring an occupational skill. The 11.4 percent of poor readers desiring education per se are men of above average intelligence with a mean IQ of 110. While only small percentages named security as the main aim in enlistment, this was in fact inherent in the desire of the majority to learn a trade. This would also appear to support the following statement in the Schools Council Working Paper No. 12 (1967) "that, asked to choose between different job characteristics, they opt for security rather than interest and for being told what to do rather than striking out on their own."

When giving reasons for enlistment, only 5 percent made some reference to the wearing of a uniform. I believe, however, that this figure does not reflect the true feelings of many of the men. A uniform endowed these men, who undoubtedly felt inferior, with a particular type of pride—"I'm good enough to be in the Army!" and they believed that people noticed them, often for the first time in their lives. This may also explain why Veness (1962) found that over a quarter of school leavers, predominantly from secondary modern schools like these soldiers, gave uniformed jobs as their first choice.

It appears from our study, therefore, that the enlistment of the majority of these men was very closely associated with a desire to obtain some form of vocational education. This evidence probably reinforces the trend toward a more realistic, work-centered curriculum for the younger pupils of the secondary schools, a factor that will assume increasing importance as more of the less able remain in school longer.

Fortunately, there are welcome signs that the more enlightened schools, aided by the research of responsible bodies, have begun to recognize the need to create in such students a greater awareness of their immediate environment and to present them with more relevant preparation for their working lives and with opportunities for work experience. The Schools' Council has shown itself to be particularly aware of this need, and the following extract from Working Paper No. 11 (1967) is particularly relevant to the young men in our study:

> Many teachers recognise the risk that the young school leaver may contract out of a school situation which is no longer of any consequence to him. His intention to leave school or his lack of academic abilities has ruled him out of a school curriculum dominated by external examinations. He feels that the school has rejected him and he rejects the school. Sympathetic teachers can see all too clearly the subsequent progress of this young school leaver and fear a rapid rejection of society in which he will be no more successful than he was in school. Acute needs, in terms of personal development, can never be satisfied by a curriculum based on a text book. What the pupil needs is the chance to learn more about himself, and more about the community in which he is to live.

LEISURE ACTIVITIES OUTSIDE THE HOME

Of the sample, 43.4 percent showed no conscious aim or serious planning in the use of their leisure time, and the majority were content with an interest in "beer and birds." This must be associated with the narrow and deprived upbringing many of them had experienced. They spent the greater part of their pay on beer and cigarettes, and very few were able to budget their money successfully even on a weekly basis.

Regarding use of leisure time when younger, 56.6 percent claimed to have attended some form of organized youth activity regularly for at least 6 months, 30.5 percent started attending but quickly lost interest, and 12.9 percent indicated no interest whatsoever in youth organizations. The majority appeared to have spent the greater part of their leisure hours roaming the streets in gangs, usually all-male groups. The gang instinct is again evidence of their need for a feeling of security and status, and as Thrasher (1927) states, it is a substitute for what society has failed to provide. The need for security, status, and a real adult relationship was evidenced by the comments of those men who attended youth organizations with some regularity:

> They was pleased to see you!
>
> The old man was in the pub all the bleeding time and my mum was all tarted up down the dance-hall so what was there at home? The chap who runs it [the Youth Club] treated me right. We talked about things and he *listened* to what I had to say. He never said, "Shut your trap about all that bleeding rubbish!"
>
> The bloke who run it, *he* never turned round and said, "What you ——— here again! Ain't you got nowhere else to go?"

Such men had found in the youth organization a sense of belonging and a warmth they had never experienced at home. Thus, work of educational value is being done in the youth service.

The distribution of attendance at youth organizations is shown in Table 4.18. It would appear from these figures that the good readers were initially more disposed than others toward taking an active interest in some form of worthwhile leisure pursuit, and also, once having become involved, their enthusiasm was more likely to be maintained over a period of time.

ANTISOCIAL BEHAVIOR

Preenlistment Crime

Of the sample, 38.8 percent were found to have been convicted of indictable offences before enlistment, while another 17.3 percent had been in trouble with authority but had not actually been convicted. The value of chi-square for the relationship between reading groups and behavior is significant at the 5 percent level (see Table 4.19). Crimes committed range from less serious charges of disturbing the peace while drunk and minor traffic offenses, to serious assault and sexual crimes. The punishment included varying amounts of fines; 25 percent of the offenders had been placed on probation. An analysis of the distribution of petty and serious crimes between the three groups of readers is shown in Table 4.20.

Approximately 65 percent of the offenders had been convicted of at least two offenses, and 17 percent, of three or more offenses. The lowest percentage (33 percent) is found among the good readers and the highest (40.7 percent) among the poor readers; within these two groups the distribution of petty and serious offenses is approximately equal.

Among the men from broken homes, the incidence of crime is 41.9 percent, which is greater than for the sample as a whole but not significantly greater than the 37.2 percent incidence for those from normal homes. The value of chi-square obtained for the relationship between the reading groups and home conditions is significant at the 1 percent level (see Table 4.21). Preenlistment crime appears to have the closest association with truancy, and 53.9 percent of habitual truants had been convicted of indictable offenses—a calculation of chi-square shows this to be significant at the 3 percent level. In many cases the tendency to crime had occurred when playing truant during hours of boredom. This study bears out the findings of Ferguson (1952) and Mays (1954) that

TABLE 4.18. Youth Organization Attendance

	P (N=140)	M (N=520)	G (N=100)	TOTAL (N=760)
Attended regularly	86 (61.4%)	271 (52.1%)	73 (73.0%)	430 (56.6%)
Started attending but fell off after 2–3 weeks	25 (17.9%)	195 (37.5%)	12 (12.0%)	232 (30.5%)
No interest	29 (20.7%)	54 (10.4%)	15 (15.0%)	98 (12.9%)

TABLE 4.19. Number Involved in PreEnlistment Crime

	P (N=140)	M (N=520)	G (N=100)	TOTAL (N=760)
Previous conviction	57 (40.7%)	205 (39.4%)	33 (33.0%)	295 (38.8%)
No previous conviction	83 (59.3%)	315 (60.6%)	67 (67.0%)	465 (61.2%)

TABLE 4.20. Distribution of Petty and Serious Crime

	P (N=140)	M (N=520)	G (N=100)	TOTAL (N=760)
Petty crime	36	117	21	174
Serious crime	21	88	12	121
TOTAL OFFENSES	57 (40.7%)	205 (39.4%)	33 (33.0%)	295 (38.8%)

TABLE 4.21. Number from Broken Homes Involved in PreEnlistment Crime

	P	M	G	TOTAL
Preenlistment crime	29	76	6	111
No preenlistment crime	28	95	31	154
TOTAL	57	171	37	265

the danger period for delinquency is between the ages of 11 and 15. Mays stated: "The falling away from delinquency appears to come after the age of fourteen when adolescence commences and awareness of individuality increases. The fact tends to confirm the view that delinquency is related to immaturity and regressive behaviour."

My study also lends support to Wiseman (1968), who cast doubt on the clinicians' approach to delinquency that stressed the importance of the home as a causative factor. The findings support those of Faris (1944), who stated "the difference in broken home rates between delinquent and non-delinquent children is little or nothing."

The following case histories not only typify the more serious crimes for which some of the men have previously been convicted but also the overall environmental situations that have predisposed them toward antisocial behavior.

CASE STUDY A

Age 19 years, A was born in Scotland, the son of an Army father and Scottish mother. When the boy was about 2 years old, the father was posted to England. The parents moved but left the child behind with his maternal grandparents where he remained until he was 10 years old. He was brought up on a 100-acre farm, and for these 8 years he was happy and apparently not worried by being apart from his real parents. He recalls being visited by them about six times. During this period the father left the Army. When the boy was 10 years old, he was taken to live with his mother and father in southeast London. He was firmly convinced that they brought him to live with them only because they could not qualify for a council home unless there was at least one child in the family living at home. Whether or not this was the reason is immaterial; their attitude toward him had utterly convinced him that this was indeed the case.

This recollection caused A to burst into tears, and he remained somewhat weepy while continuing his story. For the next 2 years his father, who worked as a male nurse in a mental hospital, often went dog racing or out with his friends in the evenings, while his mother worked at night from about 5:30 p.m. to 7:00 a.m. and then slept during the day. A was left very much to his own devices.

The father and mother quarreled frequently, often over money, the mother being beaten and reduced to tears.

When he was 12 years old, A was caught in the act of breaking and entering and placed on probation. Shortly afterward he set fire to two trucks near a factory and caused some £2,000 worth of damage. After this offense he was sent to an approved school* until he was 15 years old. After returning home from approved school, A said he was often beaten by his father for coming in late (between 10 and 11 p.m.), and his father had tried to lock him out of the house on at least one occasion.

A stated vehemently that he detested his father and had joined the Army to get away from home and to find some security. He had not visited his home in his first 10 weeks in the Army.

CASE STUDY B

B was 18 years old and had been in the Army for approximately 6 months. When B was 2 years old, his parents were divorced, and he lived with his mother, who remarried fairly quickly. He then lived with his mother and stepfather for about 8 years. His mother was again divorced and remarried very quickly. B's second stepfather was apparently an Anglo-Indian. Thus, before he was 11 years old, he had had one father and two stepfathers. He had no brothers and sisters.

The family lived in London, but the second stepfather worked and lived away from home from Mondays to Fridays. B said that he had been very unhappy with both stepfathers. He was frequently beaten by the second who appears to have been antiwhite because he himself held very strong opinions that whites are anticolored. B had several fights with this man that arose because the stepfather struck his mother. B believed his girl friend was the only person who really understood him, and she appeared to be the only stabilizing influence in his life. He admitted that he had a very quick temper and was sometimes very violent when aroused. On one occasion he had rendered his girl friend semiconscious when he nearly strangled her after a quarrel. On another occasion he had sliced open a boy's face with a broken bottle and had later smashed £25 worth of pop records. Before joining the Army he was found guilty of stealing gasoline at the garage where he worked and was fined 20 pounds and ordered to pay 56.75 pounds compensation.

---

*Approved schools were special educational establishments for young offenders. Under the Children and Young Persons Act of 1969 they became community homes.

Postenlistment Crime

The investigation shows that the men with a record of preenlistment crimes accounted for 81 percent of all military offenses and 98 percent of all civil offenses committed by the sample population during their SPE course. The only interesting feature concerning these figures is that the poor readers account for the lowest percentage of both military and civilian offenses (5.1 percent and 0.9 percent, respectively), which is the complete opposite of the findings when investigating preenlistment crime. It is difficult to prove, but I have little doubt that this change is the result of the whole approach at the school as outlined in Chapter 3: the men had found a home, warmth, understanding, and—arising from these—motivation.

It is worth recording here that during the last 18 months that I was engaged in collecting data for this study only one man was indicted by the civil courts. Considering the past records of 56.1 percent of these men, this fact is a startling tribute to the benefit obtained from the SPE course and a far greater indicator of its value in real human terms than any number of statistical tables showing increased attainments in spelling, reading, and arithmetic.

SUMMARY

From all the detail of this complex sociological study, a picture emerges of the background of the men who were to be found at the School of Preliminary Education. With but few exceptions, they were products of working class backgrounds and homes of low socio-economic status. The majority had lived mostly in large urban areas and, contrary to the often-voiced theory of many practicing educationists, had suffered little from turbulence through changes of home. In some 60 percent of the cases the mothers, despite having to cope with families well above the national average in size, had been forced by sheer economic necessity to work either part-time or full-time. The mother's efficiency in providing warmth, affection, conversation, and linguistic development at home was thus impaired, and this study finds an association between the higher-than-average proportion of working mothers and some reading difficulty.

Our research indicates that an abnormal home background is a feature closely associated with these men's general educational backwardness. The incidence of broken homes, for example, is very high, the percentage (34.9) being nearly twice that found by Morris (1966) in the

Kent Survey and by Mannheim and Wilkins (1955) in a more restricted study on borstals. Nearly one-third (32.9 percent of the students) had been accustomed to home conditions where difficult interpersonal relations disrupted their daily lives; the disruptions often ended in physical violence between members of the household. Thus the indications are that these men were the children who were discussed in the *Plowden Report* (Ministry of Education, 1967), and who did not receive special care and attention at school to compensate for the difficulties experienced at home. This finding is reinforced by the fact that for many of these men their social problems were resolved very quickly after some weeks of Service life—a life that provided the security, stability, and authority previously lacking in their environment.

An examination of the cultural standards prevailing in their homes showed a significant relationship between their reading disability, the type of reading material to which they had constantly been exposed, and the level of material they themselves purchased.

The evidence from the study fails to reveal any correlation between reading ability, class size, and number of changes of school. However, the findings concerning attitudes toward school and toward teachers are somewhat disturbing. As might be expected, there is a significant relationship between severe reading disability and an active dislike of school, but the verbal and diagnostic evidence indicates that this may well be as much the fault of inefficiency in the schools as it is that of the individual. One of the most serious findings in this study is that more than 20 percent of the men in all reading groups felt they had constantly been picked on by their teachers, that they had been labeled dull and stupid, and that the only interest their teachers had in them was that they should keep out of the way and out of trouble.

In formulating conclusions, allowances will have to be made for the many difficulties that schools are trying to solve, but the findings leave little doubt that many educationally backward pupils tend to receive considerably less sympathetic treatment and consideration at school than do their peers.

It is clear from this study that poor reading attainment is very closely associated with a poor attendance record—be the poor attendance occasioned by illness or by truancy. This confirms Wiseman's (1968) findings that "frequent absence shows a drop in reading attainment to be practically two times that of arithmetic on Mean Standard scores."

The total of 62.2 percent of men who admitted deliberately opting out of the school system is undoubtedly the most disturbing aspect of this investigation, particularly since the study also confirms that truancy is often the first step on the ladder to delinquency. The extent of truancy and the reasons expressed by 62.1 percent for joining the Army (for example, to learn a trade) focus attention on the academically oriented curricula in many of our secondary schools. Unless education can be shown to have some relevance to contemporary living, the less able pupils will continue to opt out, not only out of the school system but also out of their responsibilities as individuals and, ultimately, as citizens.

The instability and insecurity that surrounded the lives of so many of these men are shown to have been carried forward to their civilian employment records, where they experienced frequent changes of manual unskilled occupations and also of employers.

The manner in which many have just drifted into employment about which they had no knowledge gives rise to concern, and again indicates the need for an education geared to life and including "work experience." The low-grade, manual, unskilled work into which the majority had been directed or just drifted indicates the close relationship between reading/educational attainment and the probable employment prospects of the less able school leavers.

The investigation of those convicted of preenlistment crime makes dismal reading and shows delinquency to be very closely related to truancy and general educational backwardness. However, an examination of the relationship between preenlistment and postenlistment crime provides the most gratifying finding of this survey. It shows that, with sympathetic and understanding treatment, educationally backward men with previous histories of delinquency can, in a course lasting just 10½ weeks, become motivated toward self-improvement and fulfillment and develop positive attitudes toward learning and society.

CONCLUSIONS

The evidence from this study is that backwardness in reading may be caused by a number of adverse interacting environmental factors but that it cannot be attributed solely to any one factor. It is the quality of the overall social and cultural environment that is the key factor, as is so rightly stressed in the *Crowther Report* (Ministry of Education, 1960). In considering the implications of the survey, it must be remembered that an individual gets his or her education as much out of school as in, and my study indicates that academic backwardness may partly be blamed on deficiencies in the child-rearing process, inadequate child-parent relationships, and a marked lack of communication and shared interests. Many mothers, working out of sheer economic necessity or for other reasons, were not available at times of stress when they were most needed and at other times were too tired to show interest. The majority of the men in our survey, therefore, suffered from a lack of personal caring. They were the victims of early setbacks and lost ground all through the primary stage of education, until by the time the secondary stage was reached they were part of the bottom 20 percent, no matter what their innate potential.

Parental attitudes were reflected in their own attitudes toward school and the educational process, during which truancy and delinquency reached alarming proportions. However, the evidence shows that neither the schools nor the teaching profession are blameless when considering the educational state of these men. We see from their attitudes toward school and teachers, combined with their home conditions, how their educational attainments and attitudes progressively deteriorated, particularly during the secondary stage of their education.

These are factors of importance not only to schools and teachers but also to teacher training colleges, and perhaps to local government, educational, medical, and social services. One of the most disturbing findings of this investigation is that the curricula of many secondary schools do not appear to be relevant to the everyday requirements of adolescents at school and in their immediate postschool years.

The study pinpoints the need for a radical and urgent reappraisal of the aims, and consequently of the curricula, of secondary education on the lines set out in the Schools' Council Working Paper No. 11 (1967). The paper recommended that work experience be part of the curricula and subject matter be relevant to the problems found in daily life; education will thus be geared to the promotion of adult behavior patterns. The research undertaken for our enquiry shows quite clearly that the majority of our subjects were very ill-prepared in this respect and that the transition from school to community life was too abrupt and too difficult for them. They were the products of an educational system that failed to hold their interest and, more seriously, failed to help develop a sense of responsibility and a gradually increasing sense of independence—the prerequisites of a satisfactory reorientation at this critical stage in life. We must never forget that the hostility often expressed by truancy and delinquency is frequently a part of self-preservation and enters into competitive self-interest activity. It is a response to frustration and boredom.

The inference to be drawn from this study is not only that teachers need to adopt the role of the trained social worker to an increasing extent, but also that their training has left many of them inadequately prepared to meet this obligation—an obligation that will assume a proportionately greater significance as the pressures and strains imposed by the pace of modern society develop. In this context we must be able to identify those environmental factors that militate against the slow-learning to produce the underprivileged. Perhaps this study will help in their identification.

5 Ability, Development, and Attainment

If golde rust, what shall iren do?

CHAUCER

Burt (1937), having examined the factors adversely affecting the backward child, suggested that most can be categorized as either intellectual, physical, or social. The unfortunate environmental circumstances that have affected so many of the men in our survey, and hampered their educational attainment, have been discussed in detail in the previous chapter. The aim of this chapter is to examine their educational attainment and development in relation to their ability and potential, and in particular to establish whether any relationships exist between these factors and reading ability.

It is a disturbing fact that the majority of visitors to the SPE, including educationists, automatically appear to assume that the educational failure of these men is solely attributable to a lack of intelligence. In particular, there appears to be a widespread assumption that poor attainment and progress in reading are synonymous with a low intellectual capacity. This error has been perpetuated over the years in many aspects of our school system, where slow learners and those with poor social adaptation have in many instances been classified as barely educable. In spite of public concern about this problem and action by research workers and LEAs to stimulate efforts to cope with it, a surprising number of young people continue to emerge from their schooling with crippling handicaps in basic skills.

In this chapter we will try to

1. Ascertain which factors appear to be associated with failure or progress in reading

2. Examine whether any real development in academic ability or in personality took place as a result of applying the educational philosophy outlined in Chapter 3

We will also analyze the students' performances in the following tests administered before and after they completed the SPE course:

1. Attainment tests administered at the SPE
2. Army Personnel Selection tests

In addition, we will examine results obtained for two special populations from the overall sample:

1. A group of 156 men who were screened for eye defects with the cooperation of the consultant ophthalmic surgeon at the Bath Eye Infirmary
2. A group of 160 men who, before and after the SPE course, were screened on the Cornell Index—a neuropsychiatric screening test designed to differentiate persons with serious personality disturbances from the rest of the population

Details of all the tests administered are to be found in Appendix D.

INTELLIGENCE

According to Vernon (1960), intelligence is best regarded as "a fluid collection of infinitely varied thinking abilities." The days are surely past when it was regarded as a constant, and it is now generally accepted that the levels of cognitive functioning may be affected by time and by various environmental circumstances. In this situation where the majority of students had considerable difficulty in verbal skills, if intellectual assessment is to possess any degree of accuracy and be of any relevance to the formation of remedial strategies and realistic expectations, it must be obtained by means of a nonverbal test in which cognitive brightness is not obscured by verbal difficulties. The test used for this purpose was Morrisby's Compound Series Test.

The mean for the whole sample was 84.5. While this does indicate a considerable preponderance of dullness among this group, it may be due to environmental or constitutional factors, or a combination of these. However, since it has been shown in Chapter 4 that most of these men were the products of deprived environmental circumstances, perhaps there is some support here for Bowley's (1951) hypothesis that children from deprived home backgrounds are less intelligent than those living in normal homes. There is no doubt that many of these men are slow learners of less than average innate potential. In most cases, however, their learning difficulties were secondary to their emotional problems. On arrival at SPE many of them projected a false impression of utter dullness since they had given up hope. They had been schooled to accept failure and frustration.

What evidence is provided by this study to support the often-voiced theory that their reading attainment reflects their intellectual capacities? The mean nonverbal scores for the three groups of readers are set out in Table 5.1.

The striking feature of the mean scores is that they are in inverse relationship to actual measured ranges of reading ability. It is immediately apparent that the poor readers are not scoring less on tests of reading ability because they are less intelligent than either the mediocre or good readers.

The Compound Series Test does not record IQs below 65, but the percentage figures for those men who were unable to register on the scale (even after retest) are also interesting: 10.7 percent of poor readers, 11 percent of mediocre readers, and 8.5 percent of good readers.

Even more interesting are the figures for men with an IQ measured at 115 or above. These men may be described as possessing intelligence bordering on the superior. The greatest percentage of students in this category were in the group with the lowest reading attainment (4.3 percent). The mediocre readers had .58 percent; there were no men of superior intelligence in the group of good readers.

The findings of this survey, therefore, are that poor reading attainment is not necessarily indicative of low intellectual capacity; and further, it cannot be assumed that high innate potential will in itself ensure superior reading ability. Neither, of course, do these figures entitle us to an equal and opposite hypothesis—that those of low intelligence will be the most able readers. It is evident that other factors must be con-

TABLE 5.1. Mean Nonverbal Scores with Standard Deviation

READING GROUP	MEAN	S.D.
Poor	85.16	14.63
Mediocre	84.88	12.06
Good	81.77	11.65

sidered, factors that have inhibited progress and the full development of whatever potential these men possess. By an examination of their overall performance and progress on tests of attainment this study attempts to identify some of these inhibiting factors.

THE SPE TEST BATTERY

Both on arrival at the SPE and before dispersal from the course, the entire population sample was administered the following tests:

National Survey Reading Test (N.S. 6)
Holborn Reading Scale
Holborn Comprehension Test

The object of the initial testing was to ascertain the levels of attainment and establish patterns of ability and/or disability. This testing was also the first step in a continuous process of diagnosis. The general picture obtained from the initial battery was one of an all-round inferiority of attainment. Wall (1946) had obtained similar results in his studies of this type of soldier.

On the National Survey Reading Test of the NFER reading ability for the whole population sample is found to be correlated ($p < 0.001$) with performance on the SPE Spelling Test, the Holborn Reading Scale, and the Holborn Comprehension Test. These relationships are not unexpected, since reading ability is a principal factor affecting success or failure in all these tests. The correlation of the Holborn Reading Scale with the Spelling Test and its own associated Comprehension Test is also highly significant, and the connection is readily appreciated. It is surprising, however, that the results of neither of these reading tests show any significant correlation with achievement in Problem Arithmetic, where reading ability is essential to understand the problem to be solved. It is interesting that the Holborn Comprehension Test is correlated with this test to a significant degree ($p < 0.01$) thus indicating that the cognitive ability involved in comprehending the questions is perhaps similar. The Comprehension Test is correlated highly significantly with both the Spelling Test and, unexpectedly, at the 5 percent level with Mechanical Arithmetic, a test of arithmetical ability containing no verbal elements.

When the performance of the three reading groups on the initial tests is compared, we find that the relationship between performance on the different tests and reading ability diminishes as the reading attainment level increases. This appears to reflect the general level of anxiety of the poorer readers and their repeated history of frustration and failure.

In the group of poor readers, reading ability on both the NFER and Holborn tests is correlated to a highly significant degree with all the other attainments measured. In marked contrast, the reading ability of the mediocre group on the Holborn Scale is correlated only with their performance on the NFER Reading Test ($p < 0.001$) and on the Holborn Comprehension Test ($p < 0.01$). It was particularly surprising that their performance showed no correlation with the Spelling Test and with the Problem Arithmetic Test. In this group there is, however, a correlation at the 5 percent level between the NFER Reading Test and the Spelling Test.

The group of good readers shows, as might be expected, a highly significant correlation between reading ability on the Holborn Scale and Spelling Test but surprisingly shows none between the actual Reading Scale and its associated Comprehension Test. In this group reading attainment on the NFER Test is correlated only with the Holborn Comprehension Tests ($p < 0.001$). The only possible reason why this Reading Test should be correlated with the Holborn Comprehension Test, while the actual Holborn Reading Scale is not, appears to be that its design allows for a greater element of comprehension than does the oral Holborn Scale. In the NFER Test the student is required to underline the correct word from a choice of four.

The initial testing, therefore, showed that the poorer readers suffered from clusters of difficulties. The results indicate that severe reading disability must be approached as a global problem taking into account many other factors. In the case of these men it was necessary, therefore, to probe deeper through a further testing program using readily identifiable steps.

During the last week of the SPE course the students were retested on the same battery with the exception that the Schonell Mechanical and Problem Arithmetic B Tests were substituted for the A used in the initial testing. The differences found between the test results were tested for significance by the "t" test and the analysis of variance technique. The results of the "t" testing show that on all tests highly significant gains were achieved by all groups of readers taking the SPE course (see Appendix E, Table E.1). Examples of students' work before and after remedial treatment are shown in Appendix F. The course was, therefore, of considerable value to the Army even if increased academic attainment is taken as the sole criterion of its success, since such increased ability is reflected in a soldier's potential for further training.

The analysis of variance examines the results in greater depth, and it is possible to establish what differences exist between the improvements of the three groups of readers. The results of the analysis applied to the NFER Reading Test are set out in Table 5.2.

The analysis indicates that the difference between the mean improvement of the three groups on this test is highly significant. Further analysis shows that the differences between the gain in reading ability of the poor and mediocre over the good readers are highly significant. The differences in improvement between the poor and mediocre groups, however, are not significant.

The results of an analysis of variance applied to the SPE Spelling Test–Recognition are set out in Table 5.3. This analysis shows that the differences in the mean improvements of the three groups of readers are significant at the 2 percent level. An examination using "t" ratios shows that the difference in the improvement between the poor and mediocre readers is not significant. The differences between the improvement of the poor and mediocre groups over the good are significant at the 5 percent level. The greater improvements made in reading ability, and consequently in language experience, are therefore reflected in correspondingly greater improvements in the recognition of incorrectly spelled words.

An analysis of variance was also applied to the differences in improvement of the three groups on the SPE Spelling Test–Recall; the results are shown in Table 5.4.

The analysis indicates that the differences in the mean improvements between the three groups are significant at the 1 percent level. Detailed analysis shows the difference in improvement between the poor and mediocre groups to be significant at the 1 percent level, and that between the poor and good groups to be significant at the 5 percent level; the difference in the improvement between the mediocre and good groups is not significant. It is again evident, therefore, that those who have made the greatest progress in reading have made the greatest improvement in spelling, and this result might well be expected as a result of their training and improvement in analysis and synthesis.

The analysis of the improvements made in the Mechanical Arithmetic test, as shown in Table 5.5, proved surprising in that although the good readers are found to have made the greatest progress to a highly significant extent compared to either the poor or mediocre groups, the improvement of the poor readers is significantly greater than that of the mediocre group ($p < 0.05$). This result is the more surprising since this test does not depend upon any reading or linguistic skills. The explanation may be found in the overall increased ability and self-confidence

TABLE 5.2. Analysis of Variance Applied to Reading Scores (NFER Test)

READING GROUP	N	MEAN	S.D.	DF	P
Poor	140	9.100	5.685		
Mediocre	520	8.287	4.638	2	0.0001***
Good	100	6.120	4.312		

*** Highly significant

TABLE 5.3. Analysis of Variance Applied to Spelling Scores (SPE Test—Recognition)

READING GROUP	N	MEAN	S.D.	DF	P
Poor	140	8.079	7.155		
Mediocre	520	8.573	6.765	2	0.0169*
Good	100	6.510	5.030		

* Significant at 2 percent level

TABLE 5.4. Analysis of Variance Applied to Spelling Scores (SPE Test—Recall)

READING GROUP	N	MEAN	S.D.	DF	P
Poor	140	6.857	6.133		
Mediocre	520	8.892	7.178	2	0.0093**
Good	100	8.500	6.847		

** Significant at 1 percent level

TABLE 5.5. Analysis of Variance Applied to Mechanical Arithmetic Scores (Schonell)

READING GROUP	N	MEAN	S.D.	DF	P
Poor	140	5.179	3.835		
Mediocre	520	4.079	3.578	2	0.0001***
Good	100	6.690	4.079		

*** Highly significant

of the poorest readers or in the fact that the ultimate potential of the mediocre group is a limiting factor in any further achievement. The reader may well feel that perhaps another reason could be that the school was failing to motivate these students sufficiently. Since, however, they have made highly significant gains in attainment, I feel that the answer lies in a combination of the other factors we have mentioned.

Perhaps the most surprising result of all is revealed by the analysis of the Problem Arithmetic Test, as shown in Table 5.6. The differences in the mean improvements of the three groups are significant at the 5 percent level. However, although all groups made highly significant gains, the poor readers (who made such startling improvements in reading ability and in the tests so far described) failed to make any significant improvement over either the good or mediocre groups despite the fact that this is a test in which reading ability is a prerequisite of success. It appears probable that this result is linked with that of the Holborn Comprehension Test (shown later in Table 5.8), since it requires the application of cognitive skills. The mediocre readers, whose final skills in the Comprehension Test are greater than those of the poor group by nearly 50 percent, do make significantly greater progress than the good readers ($p < 0.05$).

On the Holborn Reading Scale the differences between the mean improvements of the three groups of readers are highly significant, as shown in Table 5.7. A more detailed analysis shows the improvement of the poor readers to be greater to a highly significant degree than that of both the mediocre and good groups; the improvement of the mediocre readers is greater than that of the good group to a highly significant extent. The results of this test, therefore, confirm the reading improvements shown by an analysis of the results obtained on the NFER N.S. 6 Reading Test (see Table 5.2).

It may be seen from Table 5.8 that, on the associated Holborn Comprehension Test, there is no significant difference between the improvements of any of the three reading groups, although the actual mean improvement registered by each group is highly significant. As has been stated previously, this result appears to be associated with the results of the Problem Arithmetic Test in that both require not only reading ability but also the application of cognitive skills. In comparison, the reading scales are relatively shallow in their demands. The Problem Arithmetic and Holborn Comprehension tests require the application of more penetrating cognition, and in the Comprehension Test, this must certainly be coupled with some creative skills. This is further em-

TABLE 5.6. Analysis of Variance Applied to Problem Arithmetic Scores (Schonell)

READING GROUP	N	MEAN	S.D.	DF	P
Poor	140	3.729	3.582		
Mediocre	520	3.944	3.135	2	0.0477*
Good	100	3.060	3.763		

* Significant at 5 percent level

TABLE 5.7. Analysis of Variance Applied to Reading Scores (Holborn Scale)

READING GROUP	N	MEAN	S.D.	DF	P
Poor	140	7.386	3.718		
Mediocre	520	5.873	3.366	2	0.0001***
Good	100	2.290	1.777		

*** Highly significant

TABLE 5.8. Analysis of Variance Applied to Comprehension Scores (Holborn Scale)

READING GROUP	N	MEAN	S.D.	DF	P
Poor	140	4.536	3.888		
Mediocre	520	4.600	3.562	2	0.8901*
Good	100	4.760	3.663		

* Not significant

phasized by the highly significant correlation between the performance of the poor readers on the Comprehension and Problem Arithmetic tests. Thus, despite the startling improvement made by these men in technical reading ability, their application of these newly acquired skills to tests in other areas of learning was nevertheless still limited by cognitive ability.

Summary

The analysis of performance in the SPE Test Battery thus reveals highly significant gains in level of attainment. The greatest all-round improvement was achieved by the group with the poorest reading ability. What then was happening? In a school taking great advantage of the opportunities and facilities that were available, what was limiting the overall improvement of the more able readers?

Clearly a combination of factors was operating. We have noted that on average the poor group of readers showed the greatest discrepancy between innate potential and their actual level of achievement. Thus the possibilities for improvement were greater than for the mediocre or good readers. Besides, the poorest readers, at the time of their arrival at the school, were quite unable to cope with the literary skills required in everyday life, and therefore had a far greater incentive to succeed once they were motivated. On the other hand, the better readers had sufficient skills to cope with the literacy demands of their everyday life and were therefore not so frustrated and desperate for success. It is also quite possible that the good readers, although making highly significant progress during the course, may well have approached the ceiling of their level of acquirement in basic educational skills in relation to their intellectual capacity.

THE PERSONNEL SELECTION TEST BATTERY

On joining the Army, a man undergoes a selection procedure. This procedure involves a medical examination, a series of aptitude/attainment tests, and informal interviews. The testing is to ensure that, as far as possible, a man is assigned to the most suitable employment, thus reducing to a minimum the number of failures in training. The tests are administered only by trained members of the Personnel Selection Staff under standard conditions.

In this study we are concerned with the aptitude/attainment tests and the overall Summed Selection Grading that is calculated from the results obtained on the individual tests, which are

Dominoes Non-verbal Intelligence Test
Mechanical Comprehension Test
Arithmetic Test
Test of Verbal Ability
Test of Ability to Follow Written Instructions

The Summed Selection Grading that is obtained from this test battery is of considerable importance since it is used in deciding a man's training potential. If therefore it could be established that, as a result of the SPE course, a man's overall potential for further training was increased, the school might be said to have made a very effective contribution to the Army training organization.

Nonverbal intelligence in the entire sample was found to be correlated to a highly significant degree with the Test of Ability to Follow Written Instructions and with the Summed Selection Grading. It was also correlated at the 1 percent level with the Test of Mechanical Comprehension. No significant relationship was found between nonverbal ability and the Test of Verbal Ability comprising spelling comprehension and verbal facility, nor was there any relationship with the Arithmetic Test. Thus these results indicate that intelligence is a significant factor in relation to overall training potential. They also confirm the findings from the SPE Test Battery that achievement in intelligence tests does not necessarily indicate comparable achievement in tests of verbal ability. It is a surprising fact, that although all the other tests for the overall sample and for all groups were correlated to a highly significant degree with the Summed Selection Grading, there was no significant relationship between the Test of Verbal Ability and this on initial testing. On retest no relationship was found when examined by individual groupings, but a correlation significant at the 2 percent level was found for the overall sample. Since one of the other tests was that of Ability to Follow Written Instructions, the inference here may well be that the place of the Test of Verbal Ability requires examination on the grounds that it does not contribute very much to the overall purpose of the test battery.

The initial assessment of the Personnel Selection Office (PSO) confirms the impression of all-round inferiority of attainment previously described from the results of the SPE Test Battery.

Soldiers who attended the SPE course were retested on the PSO Battery after return to their units and the results were forwarded to the school for information. The differences found between the results of the two sets of test scores were tested for significance by the "t" test and the analysis of variance technique. The results of the "t" testing show that on all tests highly significant gains were achieved by all groups of readers during the SPE course (see Appendix E, Table E.2). In addition, and more important for the Army training organization, the testing showed a highly significant gain for all the groups in the Summed Selection Gradings. Thus, in a 10½ week course, the employment and training potential of these soldiers was radically improved.

The test results were examined in greater depth by analysis of variance to establish what differences might exist between the improvements of the three groups of readers. The results of the analysis applied to the Nonverbal Intelligence Test are set out in Table 5.9.

TABLE 5.9. Analysis of Variance Applied to Nonverbal Intelligence Test (PSO Battery)

READING GROUP	N	MEAN	S.D.	DF	P
Poor	140	4.086	5.683		
Mediocre	520	3.613	5.413	2	0.0065**
Good	100	5.490	4.927		

** Significant at 1 percent level

The analysis indicates that the differences between the mean improvements for the three reading groups are significant at the 1 percent level. Further analysis by "t" ratios shows the improvement of the good readers to be significantly greater than that of the poor group at the 5 percent level, and to be greater than that of the mediocre readers to a highly significant degree. The difference in improvement between the poor and mediocre readers is not significant. These results lend some support to Vernon (1961) who contends that "the brains do get rusty from lack of practice" and perhaps also to his statement that "the most able retain their intelligence best." Although a greater improvement in nonverbal ability was shown by the good readers in this particular test, we must remember that it is the poor readers who do advance considerably in reading attainment. Thus, we cannot expect a rise in nonverbal scores always to be associated with improvement in reading ability.

The results of an analysis of variance applied to the results of the Mechanical Comprehension Test are set out in Table 5.10. This analysis shows that the differences between the mean improvements of these three groups of readers are significant at the 5 percent level. Application of "t" ratios show that the improvement of the good readers is significantly greater than that of the poor group at the 2 percent level. The differences in improvement between the good and mediocre readers and the poor and mediocre readers are not significant. This result reflects the findings of the analysis of variance applied to the SPE tests, which show that the good readers make their greatest improvements in tests requiring the application of cognitive skills.

Table 5.11 sets out the results when an analysis of variance was applied to the Arithmetic Test. The analysis indicates that the differences between the improvements of the three reading groups are significant at the 5 percent level. Detailed analysis shows the improvement of the good readers to be significantly greater than that of the poor group ($p < 0.01$) and also than that of the mediocre readers ($p < 0.05$). The

TABLE 5.10. Analysis of Variance Applied to Mechanical Comprehension (PSO Battery)

READING GROUP	N	MEAN	S.D.	DF	P
Poor	140	2.643	4.100		
Mediocre	520	3.038	4.497	2	0.0631*
Good	100	3.990	4.914		

* Significant at 5 percent level

TABLE 5.11. Analysis of Variance Applied to Arithmetical Scores (PSO Battery)

READING GROUP	N	MEAN	S.D.	DF	P
Poor	140	5.207	5.341		
Mediocre	520	5.792	5.024	2	0.0289*
Good	100	6.980	5.516		

* Significant at 5 percent level

TABLE 5.12. Analysis of Variance Applied to Verbal Ability (PSO Battery)

READING GROUP	N	MEAN	S.D.	DF	P
Poor	140	5.00	5.252		
Mediocre	520	4.779	5.483	2	0.0303*
Good	100	6.400	6.779		

* Significant at 5 percent level

TABLE 5.13. Analysis of Variance Applied to Ability to Follow Written Instructions (PSO Battery)

READING GROUP	N	MEAN	S.D.	DF	P
Poor	140	19.907	15.659		
Mediocre	520	14.248	13.414	2	0.0001***
Good	100	13.370	12.475		

*** Highly significant

difference between the improvement of the poor and mediocre readers is not statistically significant. This result is a complete reversal of that obtained on the Schonell Mechanical Arithmetic Test in the SPE battery. A further factor affecting this result and the greater improvement of the most able readers is that the PSO test does involve simple mechanical arithmetical calculations, and thus there is a need to apply cognitive skills. It would appear, therefore, that this result corroborates the findings of the analysis of improvements on the Schonell Problem Arithmetic Test.

When an analysis of variance was applied to the differences in the improvement of the three groups of readers on the Test of Verbal Ability, the results were as shown in Table 5.12. The differences in the mean improvements between the three reading groups are significant at the 5 percent level. The difference in improvement between the good and mediocre readers is significant at the 1 percent level; the differences in improvement between the good and poor readers and the poor and mediocre groups are not significant. Thus the results of this analysis might well have been predicted by an examination of the Holborn Comprehension test results, which confirmed that the application of technical reading skills to other areas of learning is limited by cognitive ability.

Set out in Table 5.13 are the results of an analysis of variance applied to the test of Ability to Follow Written Instructions. The analysis shows the differences in the mean improvements between the three reading groups to be highly significant. Further analysis shows the improvement of the good readers to be greater than that of the poor group to a highly significant degree; the same can be said of the improvement of the poor readers over the mediocre. The difference in the improvement between the good and mediocre readers is not significant. Again, this analysis appears to substantiate the findings of the SPE Battery. This test, as with the Schonell Problem Arithmetic Test and the Holborn Comprehension Test, requires not only reading ability but also the application of cognitive skills in carrying out complex instructions rapidly and accurately.

Table 5.14 gives the results of an analysis of variance applied to the differences between the improvements of the three groups of readers on the Summed Selection Gradings. The analysis indicates that the differences between the mean improvements of the three groups are highly significant. Further analysis shows the improvement of the good readers to be significantly greater than that of the poor group ($p < 0.01$). The improvement of the good readers is greater to a highly significant

TABLE 5.14. Analysis of Variance Applied to the Summed Selection Grading (PSO Battery)

READING GROUP	N	MEAN	S.D.	DF	P
Poor	140	−2.707	1.841		
Mediocre	520	−2.571	1.791	2	0.0001***
Good	100	−3.470	1.749		

*** Highly significant

TABLE 5.15. Students Claiming Previous Eye Trouble

COMPLAINT	P	M	G	TOTAL
Eye trouble only	28	75	15	118
Eye and ear trouble	4	4	1	9
Eye and speech trouble	3	16	6	25
TOTAL	35	95	22	152

degree than that of the mediocre group. The difference between the improvements of the poor and mediocre readers is not significant. The all-round greater improvements achieved by good readers in the PSO Battery are indicated in this analysis of overall selection grading.

Summary

The picture emerging from the analysis of performance on the PSO Test Battery is that of highly significant gains in levels of aptitude/attainment. However, in marked contrast to the results obtained in the SPE Battery of academic attainment tests, it was the good readers who produced the greater all-round improvement. Thus, the PSO Test results provide an answer to the suggestion that the school failed to motivate good readers sufficiently. One can also conclude that training potential and job suitability are best indicated by reading ability together with comprehension skills. The analysis also indicates that intelligence is closely associated with training potential. Since all the reading groups made highly significant gains in all the tests, and therefore in the Summed Selection Gradings, the results of this analysis indicate clearly that the SPE course made a considerable contribution to the training potential available within the Army. The experience with the SPE program should also provide encouragement when considering the problems of retraining in the civilian world.

OPHTHALMIC DEFECTS, LATERALITY, AND READING ABILITY

The information gained by instructors when completing the Personal Interview Proforma indicated that one out of every five students had previously suffered from eye troubles. A breakdown of the distribution of numbers between the reading groups is shown in Table 5.15.

In their reading and writing many of the men showed difficulty in left/right orientation, which was revealed in reversals and rotational difficulties with such letters as "u" and "n." It was clear that some were uncertain about their own laterality, and among the poor reading groups, there were many with inadequate spatial orientation in the application of laterality to external objects. In addition to this, there always appeared to be a large percentage of men complaining of headaches, eyeaches, and watering eyes when faced with tasks involving reading or writing. Undoubtedly, there were some psychosomatic symptoms appearing in conjunction with the need to tackle difficult tasks. However, some who from previous history should have been wearing glasses, which had been prescribed and issued through the Schools Medical Service, said they had been prevented from wearing them either by direct parental influence or by parental and family ridicule. Typical of this is the statement made by a soldier who was subsequently found to require glasses to correct astigmatism: "When I came home with my glasses my Dad said, 'What you want with these things, you four-eyed nit? I never wore no glasses nor my Dad before me. Anybody'd think you was clever. Well, *we* know you ain't so don't be so stupid!' "

It should be noted at this point that all the recruits to the Army, apart from a few special categories, are now processed through the Recruit Selection Centre at Sutton Coldfield. In this centralized system far more rigid medical standards are applied by R.A.M.C. personnel than was possible under the old system, and it is unlikely that so many men with uncorrected eye difficulties would escape detection. However, because of a visit by a soldier to the Bath Eye Infirmary, the consultant ophthalmic surgeon, Mr. T. Kelly, F.R.C.S., became interested in our particular problem. We were then able to establish a system of eye screening in conjunction with the infirmary, to examine what relationships, if any, existed between eye defects and reading disability. A checklist of factors to be examined, both at the SPE and the Infirmary, was devised and is reproduced in full in Appendix G, Table G.1.

In this investigation a total of 160 men were screened in groups of 25–30 within 2 or 3 days of their arrival at the school. The 160 men were divided into reading groups on the criteria used throughout this study. The distribution between the three reading groups is poor readers, 31; mediocre readers, 104; and good readers, 25.

In that part of the screening carried out at the SPE, reading age was based upon the Holborn Scale and IQ on the nonverbal Compound Series Test used in the SPE Test Battery. Dominance was examined using the Harris Tests of Lateral Dominance. Clinical examination supplemented by discussion suggested that many of the men may have suffered from confused lateral dominance in their early years and later settled into crossed dominance. Certainly my own investigation had indicated that those who had previously suffered from confused laterality and those suffering from it at the school had very poor orientation to words and a high proportion used right to left eye movements.

The theory of hemispherical dominance and its relationship with laterality has occupied psychologists, neurologists, and educationists for many years. The evidence on the effects of lateral dominance on reading ability is very confused, with many researchers making unequivocal statements that a direct relationship exists and others flatly claiming that it does not.

Parson (1924) has suggested that all actions are hampered unless the dominant hand and eye are on the same side of the body. This theory finds some support from Schonell (1942), who found that in a group of backward readers 52 percent suffered from crossed dominance. MacMeeken (1942), in a study of 140 retarded children, found the incidence of left-eyedness was 58.6 percent as compared with 37.28 percent in the normal population. Monroe (1932) had also presented evidence that crossed laterality of hand and eye is the disturbing factor and that left-eyedness with right-hand preference was significantly greater with defective readers than with their controls.

On the other hand Bond and Tinker (1967) cite situations that show no relationship between laterality and reading disability. Gates and Bond (1936) also found no significant difference in the incidence of laterality between matched groups of retarded and normal readers. Trieschman's (1968) findings are interesting since she found that only those children with IQs of less than 125 showed any association between laterality and reading disability.

The most balanced views on this whole subject are those of Zangwill (1962) and Anthony (1968). Zangwill, while asserting that those with severe reading disability (i.e., dyslexia) do show poorly developed laterality, also questioned why all ill-lateralized children are not backward in reading. Anthony examined the interrelationship of factors in a study of cerebral dominance and reading disability, using the Harris Tests of Lateral Dominance on dyslexic and nondyslexic children. He also studied perceptual development and directionality, and concluded that while mixed dominance by itself cannot be regarded as a predictor of reading performance, it may be regarded as one of several factors that jointly may affect reading performance.

Before discussing the findings of our intensive eye screening experiment, I want to mention the invaluable assistance given in the sphere of laterality by the regimental NCOs responsible for drill and physical training. They reported such signs as lack of rhythm when marching, uncertainty in the execution of left/right orders, awkwardness in physical movement or gait, and balancing difficulties. There was a highly significant correlation between these reports and the incidence of men with crossed laterality. Thus again the evidence from this study indicates the need to approach diagnosis of educational difficulties from a global viewpoint in order to reach any meaningful conclusions.

A complete list of the variables checked and a breakdown of the numbers and percentages found in each of the three reading groups is shown in Appendix G, Table G.2. The figures from this sample (item 1 in the table) confirm the findings of the sociological investigation reported in Chapter 4—that adverse environmental factors are significantly associated with poor reading attainment.

Of the sample, 22.5 percent were right-handed and left-eyed. The distribution of the numbers with this feature among the reading groups is set out in item 3 of Table G.2. It is interesting to compare the wide variation of numbers within reading groups, shown in item 3, with the even distribution of right-handed and right-eyed students, shown in item 2. The figures confirm the findings of Monroe (1932) that crossed laterality of hand and eye is a disturbing factor in reading development and also that left-eyedness with right-hand preference is significantly greater among the poorer readers.

Some factors that stand out in the statistics in Table G.2 are not unexpected. There are significant differences in number in the reading groups among those who reverse letters, those who mix the order of letters in words, those who produce a bizarre order of letters, those whose hearing/writing transfer is poor, and those who exhibit symptoms of neurological difficulty. All these factors are associated with very poor reading ability. In instances of neurological difficulty and the writing of letters in words in a bizarre order, it is significant that no cases are to be found among the good readers.

One of the most disturbing features of this investigation is the overall incidence (21.9 percent) of men who confessed that they had previously worn glasses but no longer did so. In later discussion this will be shown to be a factor closely connected with overall reading ability, but it is not significantly different in respect of the poor readers. Perhaps the most important finding of this experiment was the overall number of men who were discovered to be in need either of glasses or of orthoptic exercises because of defective visual acuity. The distribution of numbers between the reading groups is set out in Table 5.16.

The value of chi-square obtained for the relationship between the three groups is highly significant ($p < 0.001$). Thus, as one might have expected, a clear relationship is shown to exist between poor reading ability and defective visual acuity.

The investigation shows the main defects of sight to be hypermetropia (farsightedness), myopia (nearsightedness), astigmatism, and convergence insufficiency. All these defects have implications for reading and the ready identification of symbols. Hypermetropia and myopia are conditions that describe errors of refraction. In each case a blurred image, large in myopia and small in hypermetropia, is formed on the retina and vision is impaired. In hypermetropia the eyes have not yet come to focus for close work such as the 25-centimeter distance for reading under normal conditions; in myopia, on the other hand, a defect of 4 dioptres means that the far point of distant vision is only 25 centimeters. After this point is reached, the focus commences to diverge, and difficulties are encountered. Hypermetropia is often the basis of the common squint and gives rise to symptoms such as aching of the eyes and "gritty" feeling, and is associated with headache over and around the eye.

Astigmatism is irregular curvature of the eye that prevents it from focusing properly and results in distortion or blurred vision. People with this eye condition see shapes that have no clarity, and it therefore affects reading.

Convergence insufficiency produces symptoms of defective fusion. There are difficulties in distinguishing symbols in close work because the eyes cannot fuse an image adequately at short range. This makes reading difficult. Convergence insufficiency is frequently accompanied by headaches, and the condition is corrected either by using glasses or through orthoptic exercises.

The incidence of defective visual acuity confirms the findings of the Optical Information Council (1968). In a random survey of 1,000 school children it found that one in four had eye faults. This survey also discovered nearsightedness to be the most common defect.

The figures in Table G.2 (items 43–45) also show the substantial proportion in each reading group who complained of headache, eyeache, and eye pain and discomfort; 38.7 percent of the poor group, 43.4 percent of the mediocre group, and 60 percent of the good group.

TABLE 5.16. Defective Visual Acuity Among the Reading Groups

VISUAL ACUITY	P	M	G	TOTAL
Defective	23	22	6	51
Not defective	8	82	19	109
TOTAL	31	104	25	160

It is to be expected that many of those with astigmatism or convergence insufficiency would have suffered frequently from headaches and/or eye discomfort. The investigation revealed, however, that the number of men with headaches plus ocular abnormalities and defective visual acuity was not significantly different from the number with headaches and no ocular abnormalities or defective visual acuity. This appears to support our belief that many of the headaches were psychosomatic in nature, probably originating in anxiety. An interesting fact about the headaches with no ocular abnormality is that they were described as having been present for years and associated with moving objects such as television, cinema, reading, and glare, the glare invariably occurring out of doors while the man was moving. The reported position of the headache—eyes or temporal—is very much the same (60–40 percent) for the groups with or without ocular abnormality.

From our reexamination of the cases where no ocular abnormality existed, it was found that there were no instances of similar complaint while traveling by bus, train, or car. This gives added weight to our hypothesis concerning the psychosomatic basis of the headaches.

The information accumulated from the screening process, together with the reading ages and IQs of the students concerned, was subjected to regression analysis. The object of this analytical procedure was to establish which, if any, of the factors examined appeared to be most relevant to reading attainment. It is also possible from this analysis to predict the reading age of any individual in the sample by using the eye data variables and the coefficient in the appropriate formula.

The factors listed in descending order of importance in Table 5.17 are those that have the closest connection with reading attainment. In a regression analysis the factors in a summary table are interrelated; for example, astigmatism has a significant relationship with reading ability, and it is only fourth in order of importance if the preceding three factors have been taken into account.

This table shows the greatest predictor of poor reading ability to be the writing of letters in words in a bizarre order. This variable has a highly significant negative correlation with reading attainment, thus in-

TABLE 5.17. Step-wise Multiple Regression Analysis—Summary Table

VARIABLE	MULTIPLE R	MULTIPLE R^2	F TO REMOVE
Order of letters in written words bizarre	0.3753	0.1408	25.077
Adverse home circumstances	0.4281	0.1833	7.903
IQ	0.4724	0.2232	7.760
Astigmatic	0.5111	0.2612	7.711
Hear/write transfer very weak	0.5495	0.3020	8.702
Mixed dominance—right-handed/left-eyed	0.5720	0.3272	5.563
History of previous glasses	0.5924	0.3510	5.373
Headache/eyeache in crowds	0.6149	0.3781	6.363
Convergence insufficiency	0.6283	0.3948	4.006

dicating that the more this feature is in evidence the lower will be the level of reading ability.

The analysis confirms the findings from the sociological examination of the large sample in Chapter 4 that adverse home circumstances are to be significantly associated with reading ability ($p < 0.01$). This again is negatively correlated, showing this factor to be of increasing importance as reading attainment levels decrease. Our investigation confirms, too, the previous finding that IQ, which is significantly correlated with reading ability ($p < 0.01$), is not the most useful predictor of attainment in this field.

Astigmatism shows a correlation with reading attainment at the 2 percent level when variations in reading age have been made with respect to the preceding factors named in Table 5.17. In my opinion the figure does not indicate the true importance of this variable in reading attainment. Table G.2 (Appendix G) shows this ocular abnormality to be present in 42.5 percent of the sample. When this percentage is related to the fact that the mean reading age for the experimental population is only 10 years 4 months, the position of this variable becomes more realistic.

The mean reading age quotient suggests that the sample included many men whose hearing/writing transfer was poor. This variable is correlated to a highly significant degree with reading ability. The correlation is negative, indicating an increasing association as the level of reading attainment decreases. An examination of the numbers that have this difficulty in the three reading groups shows the differences between the groups to be highly significant.

Mixed dominance with preference for the left eye and right hand is significantly associated with reading ability ($p < 0.05$), a negative correlation showing an increasing relationship as the level of reading attainment decreases.

Thus, this analysis enables us to pick out the factors most relevant to reading, and if we use them as predictors, a very fair correspondence with reading age may be obtained.

Summary

The evidence from this study in conjunction with the Bath Eye Infirmary lends support to the views of Schonell (1942) and Monroe (1932) that reading ability is hampered by crossed laterality, particularly by crossed laterality of right hand and left eye. The views of Bond and Tinker (1967) that there is no relationship between laterality and reading ability are not supported by this statistical evidence. This study, however, does not suggest that crossed laterality by itself can be utilized to explain reading failure, but it does appear from the principal component analysis to be a precipitating factor. Thus, this experiment confirms Anthony's (1968) findings that crossed laterality is one of a number of important manifestations in a reading disability syndrome; it is a part of the global difficulties of the retarded reader.

This study also shows the incidence of defective visual acuity to be significantly high among our group of poor achievers, particularly so among the poorest readers. There is a disturbing percentage of men (23.3) for whom glasses had been prescribed during their schooldays and who clearly had been retarded educationally by a failure, frequently on the part of parents, to accept the need for these.

Since almost as many men without ocular abnormalities as with them indicated frequent eyeaches and headaches, it follows that a considerable number suffered from psychosomatic symptoms; these symptoms reflected the general high level of anxiety pervading their lives.

The investigation does not suggest that the visual defects discovered inhibit reading completely, but it may well be that they are, as Wall (1946) stated, sensory defects that "operate as a distraction slightly increasing the gap between the ability to 'bark at print' and the 'ability to understand the bark.' "

EMOTIONAL AND PERSONALITY DISORDERS

Over the years researchers have generally agreed that a deprived environment is prognostic of educational and/or emotional difficulties. Smith (1955) in a survey of literature on this subject found many emotional maladjustments to stem from the home. Bowlby (1956), in discussing deprived children, pointed out that personality difficulties are among characteristics that can be attributed to the effects of deprivation itself. It is obvious, therefore, from the information discussed in Chapter 4, that many men in this sample were likely to be suffering from emotional strain or personality disorders. We should now consider what emotional factors previous researchers have found to be associated with reading difficulties.

Siegel (1954) found reading disability to be frequently accompanied by personality maladjustment but stated that there is no "typical" personality pattern that is characteristic of reading failure. Witty and Kopel (1939) reported that some 50 percent of seriously retarded readers attending the Northwestern University Psycho-Educational Clinic had "fears and anxieties so serious and so far-reaching that no programme of re-education could possibly succeed which did not aim to re-establish self-confidence and to remove anxieties."

In the opinion of Gates (1941), emotional and personality problems are present in about 75 percent of retarded readers, but he felt that in only about one quarter of them is it the actual cause of the disability. Gates also drew attention to a statement by Chatfield, Director of Attendance and Child Welfare for New York City, who was convinced that "the continual frustration in school produced by inability to read efficiently frequently led to truancy and delinquency." This statement made in 1941 could well have been prepared to describe the sample under discussion. Robinson (1946), Holmes (1955), Blanchard (1928), Monroe (1932), Burt (1955), and Schonell (1942) all draw attention to the emotional concomitants of reading disability.

In general, all the researchers find anxiety to be a strongly inhibiting factor. Morris (1966) and Burt (1955) are among those who find a significant correlation between anxiety and reading disability. Morris in the Kent Survey stated that "many poor readers become withdrawn, depressed, anxious."

Although most authorities agree on the pressure of emotional difficulties and, in particular, of anxiety in reading disability, few will offer firm opinions as to cause and effect. This is hardly surprising and is borne out by this study. So many factors need to be considered that, in most cases, it was quite impossible to ascertain whether anxiety reaction was "the chicken or the egg." If reading failure creates emotional maladjustment, which inhibits further learning, then in some cases we are likely to find even greater emotional difficulties. Emotional difficulties have, in some instances, prevented a man from learning to read; in others, they have prevented him from using the reading ability he possesses; and in a few serious cases, they have made a man inaccessible to reading instruction. It is possible only to make one categorical statement about these difficulties. They must be recognized, faced, and coped with in a rational way. This point was emphasized by Sherman (1939) who stated that "emotions must be taken into account in evaluating success and failure." He went on to state that emotional balance or imbalance will understandably affect retention, recall, and the transfer of learning and that "whatever therapeutic programme is instituted, the initial step must be an evaluation of the emotional pattern."

The men with whom we are concerned failed not only in reading but also in life. Educational failure pervaded their whole personalities; the backward adult comes to accept this frustration as an inevitable fact of life. As Wall (1946) discovered, part of the all-round inferiority of the backward reader is in emotional instability. Any existing emotional difficulties are likely, therefore, to have become exacerbated and not alleviated by time. The educational therapy required was thus one by which it was hoped to modify attitudes to work and to training. This approach has been discussed in Chapter 3.

Those working at SPE were utterly convinced that the greatest achievement of the SPE course was giving the student confidence in his own ability and improving his attitudes and social adaptation so that he could become a better and more contented soldier and citizen. Many senior officers and commanding officers of units from which students were drawn supported this view, as did PSOs in their reports on retesting. Two extracts illustrate this point quite clearly. The first is from a letter to the SPE from a senior officer in the Ministry of Defence:

> The atmosphere between instructors and soldiers struck me as being quite excellent and this is obviously what has been the main reason for your success. The individual teaching techniques are so successful in bringing on these backward young men and this gives them the confidence in their own ability to make them reasonable soldiers.

The second extract is from a typical report written by a PSO on retesting:

> This man has a new confidence in his own ability to make a success of his Army life. He seems more alert and generally more alive.

These were subjective impressions, however, and no statistical evidence to substantiate our claim was available. In any event was it really possible to make any significant modification of ingrained attitudes and emotional problems in a 10½ week course? Were we perhaps buoyed up by false hopes and delusions of educational grandeur?

It was decided, therefore, to attempt an objective evaluation of personalities both at the beginning and at the end of the SPE course and to subject the findings to statistical analysis. The Cornell Index, a neuropsychiatric screening test developed originally for the U.S. Army and modified for civilian use, was administered to the same group of men (160) who took part in the eye experiment. The Cornell Index (see Appendix D) consists of 101 questions referring to neuropsychiatric and psychosomatic symptoms that are grouped as follows:

1. Defects in adjustment expressed as feelings of fear and inadequacy
2. Pathological mood reactions, especially depression
3. Nervousness and anxiety
4. Neurocirculatory psychosomatic symptoms
5. Pathological startle reactions
6. Other psychosomatic symptoms
7. Hypochondriasis and asthenia
8. Gastrointestinal psychosomatic symptoms
9. Excessive sensitivity and suspiciousness
10. Troublesome psychopathy

The Index is predominantly concerned with indicating the presence of anxiety states and associated disorders; the groups of items obviously cannot be regarded in isolation. The Index has a record of success in this role, and it was for this reason that it was selected as an adjunct to the clinical interview. It must be emphasized here that we were not looking for psychotic conditions in these soldiers but rather indications of the nature of their neuroses, which are concerned with what Burt (1955) calls the "personal" emotions and are due largely to the unfortunate environmental conditions during childhood that had an inhibiting effect upon performance and potential. The neurologist Ernest Jones (1920) states that "neuroses are the outcome of the conflict between the individual and society"; they are the result of maladjustment between the individual and his total environment. There is no organic disease and the symptoms are devoid of any easily discernible cause. Burt, in common with many researchers, finds anxiety to be particularly prevalent among delinquents and truants, and this is given support by the high incidence of previous crime and truancy among these men (see Chapter 4).

General Characteristics of the Sample

Before discussing the results of this testing, it is perhaps appropriate to describe the general characteristics of these men. The majority were youthful and immature, physically as well as mentally underdeveloped for their ages. They were tied to direct and immediate sensory expression. In communication much use was made of gestures and facial expression to assist language. They were also immature in that they found great difficulty in persevering with any one activity or problem. They lacked concentration and were often listless and apathetic when they first arrived. The poorer the performance in reading, the poorer I found to be the self-image concept. In some, of course, a fear of their own inadequacy led to boasting and displays of aggressive behavior patterns. Even from subjective impressions alone, it was evident that the greater the discrepancy between intelligence and reading attainment, the greater was the emotional difficulty, since such men had become increasingly aware of their own limitations.

Personality development involves the learning of roles that may be seen as a series of developmental tasks to be accomplished if an individual is to adjust to the society in which he lives. It is in this aspect of their lives that these men had the greatest failure. They were not entirely dull, however, and underlying the apprehension or bravado there was often more sensitivity and spirituality than they were able or prepared to express openly.

In accordance with the findings in *Comprehensive Schools in Action* (Cole, 1964), the men in our sample tended to choose their friends from among students in the same ability, behavioral, and ethnic groups. They usually selected girl friends and wives who would be able to make the major decisions of life. In this they appeared to be repeating the pattern of life to which many were accustomed as children: 88.8 percent of those who during childhood had both parents alive and cohabiting regarded the mother as the decision maker and the dominant figure in the household. Their need for human warmth and a sense of security was evident from the number with the fantasy of an ideal, loving, and caring wife—the "happily ever after" fairy story ending to their problems. In the same way the decision to join the Army was a reflection of basic emotional needs. Their adjustment at the SPE became a major aspect of their general adjustment to life, and they had selected a pattern of life to satisfy their needs.

The results of the initial screening on the Index indicate that on arrival at the SPE 60.6 percent were suffering from emotional problems that were likely to inhibit their learning potential and/or actual job performance. The prevalent disorder was that of an immature or inadequate personality together with associated anxiety. This finding was not surprising and is symptomatic of those whose lives exhibit a long pattern of failure and frustration and a consequent inability to cope adequately with the demands of everyday living. In such persons there is often a wide discrepancy between their actual levels of attainment and the capacities they seem to have. They have failed to develop mature emotional and motivational patterns. Their behavior is characterized by poor judgment and general ineptitude; energy and drive are low, and the whole life pattern shows a lack of foresight, planning, and perseverance. The Index confirmed the dependency needs that have already been noted in their relationships with women and the Army; thus the investigation confirmed their need for the support of favorable environmental conditions. In fact, 75.5 percent expressed a desire for someone always to be on hand to give help and assistance.

The presence of chronic anxiety is also indicated by the number of men exhibiting associated nervous disorders: stammering, 15 percent; previous asthmatic conditions, 5 percent; previous nervous disability/breakdown, 5 percent; history of fits in childhood, 6.9 percent; and insomnia, 27.5 percent. Anxiety is also reflected in those sections of the Index that cover fear and inadequacy, and sensitivity and suspiciousness; and for the whole sample the correlation of anxiety with all the other subsections of the test is highly significant. Surprisingly the mediocre readers showed the highest level of anxiety, and for the overall sample, this is correlated to a highly significant degree with all other sections of the Index.

The high levels of anxiety are easily understood when the following case studies are considered.

CASE STUDY C

A very willing and pleasant youth of reasonable innate ability, C showed an IQ of 98 on the Compound Series Test. He arrived at the SPE as a total illiterate. Born and brought up in County Dublin, he was the victim of a most distressing environmental situation, being removed from school completely when he was 10 years old in order to go and work with his father in the fishing boats. Previously he had attended school spasmodically when his father did not need him for work. The father, the picture of a proverbial drunkard, attempted to "educate" him by physical force. He was placed at a table with reading books and every error was cruelly punished by the use of a leather strap, boot, gun butt, or fist. As a result, the learning situation became completely associated with fear and physical violence. Suffering from chronic anxiety, fear, and inadequacy, he made little progress in 4½ months even with the constant individual instruction available in the Remedial Centre. Any form of close supervision produced psychosomatic symptoms such as flushing, profuse perspiration, and rapid pulse. He had suffered from severe pains in the head since the age of 13, when he was hit on the head by his father with a 1-pound hammer. He had also fallen off a motor cycle on to the top of his head when he was 15 years old but did not seek medical attention.

Because of his environmental association with a drunken father and violence, he loathed alcohol and had a marked tendency to go berserk when one of his roommates came in drunk.

He became worried that he was losing his memory, and there was, in fact, a marked regression in his powers of retention. He brooded a lot and appeared to have become obsessed with a desire to get even with his father by going home to thrash him. This was perfectly understandable since we learned that while C was at the SPE, the father had knocked the mother down a flight of stairs and she had broken her arm.

He suffered from frequent headaches and eyeache and the local optician prescribed glasses for myopia.

It was necessary to refer the man for psychiatric examination, and he was medically discharged from the Army. The psychiatrist felt that it would be dangerous for C to return home. In consequence, he was given a job as a civilian at the SPE and he continued to adjust slowly to his new life.

CASE STUDY D

This soldier was a pleasant, clean-looking youth with an IQ in the upper average range. He had a reading age of 10 years 6 months and was referred to the SPE because of an inability to pass the Army Certificate of Education, Third Class. His commanding officer was of the opinion that his educational backwardness was creating behavioral problems since he had begun to display antisocial tendencies.

On arrival at the SPE, D showed considerable nervousness and appeared very startled and apprehensive when addressed. He had evidently lost all confidence in his own ability to tackle the most elementary comprehension and free writing exercises. He had become extremely resentful and suspicious of any comment and advice. Also, he did not associate freely with his fellows as was the general pattern.

However, he possessed considerable imagination. A further contrast with his fellows was provided by the idealistic moral attitudes that he propounded. He was forever composing letters to the BBC about the content and standards of their programs. This man was the third of four siblings. His father had been blinded in World War II and was in very poor health, and his mother died when he was just 5 years old. He was brought up by his maternal grandmother, father, and eldest sister. He was also sent to an orphanage for 18 months.

He stated that he was always very frightened as a child and described his eldest sister as being "very nervous." He scored high on the Cornell Index, which revealed manifest anxiety and a variety of psychosomatic symptoms. An investigation revealed other associated disorders—stammering, enuresis until the age of 7, and chronic nail biting.

His family had a history of left-handedness, twinning, and speech-reading difficulties. He showed incomplete lateralization and all these features, and educational testing supported a diagnosis of dyslexia. A specimen of his written work on arrival is shown in Figure 5.1.

He responded well to a structured program of phonic work and counseling and improved his reading ability by more than 3 years. His self-confidence was built up, and his anxiety decreased markedly. He was able to pass his examination for Army Certificate of Education, Third Class, and when last heard of he was an NCO with his unit, displaying an ability to accept responsibility.

The influence of environmental factors on emotional attitudes was clearly shown when projective methods were used calling for spontaneous response associations. Below are two examples of typical responses from soldiers on the Rotter Incomplete Sentence Test; the responses are italicized.

EXAMPLE 1

I feel *like I'm unwanted.*
My nerves *are very bad indeed.*
I suffer *a lot from headaches and pains.*
The only trouble *is I don't want to go home.*
People *are always staring at me.*
I need *all the help I can get.*
Reading *I'm very bad at.*
In school *I never learned anything.*

FIGURE 5.1. Writing of Case Study D on arrival at the SPE.

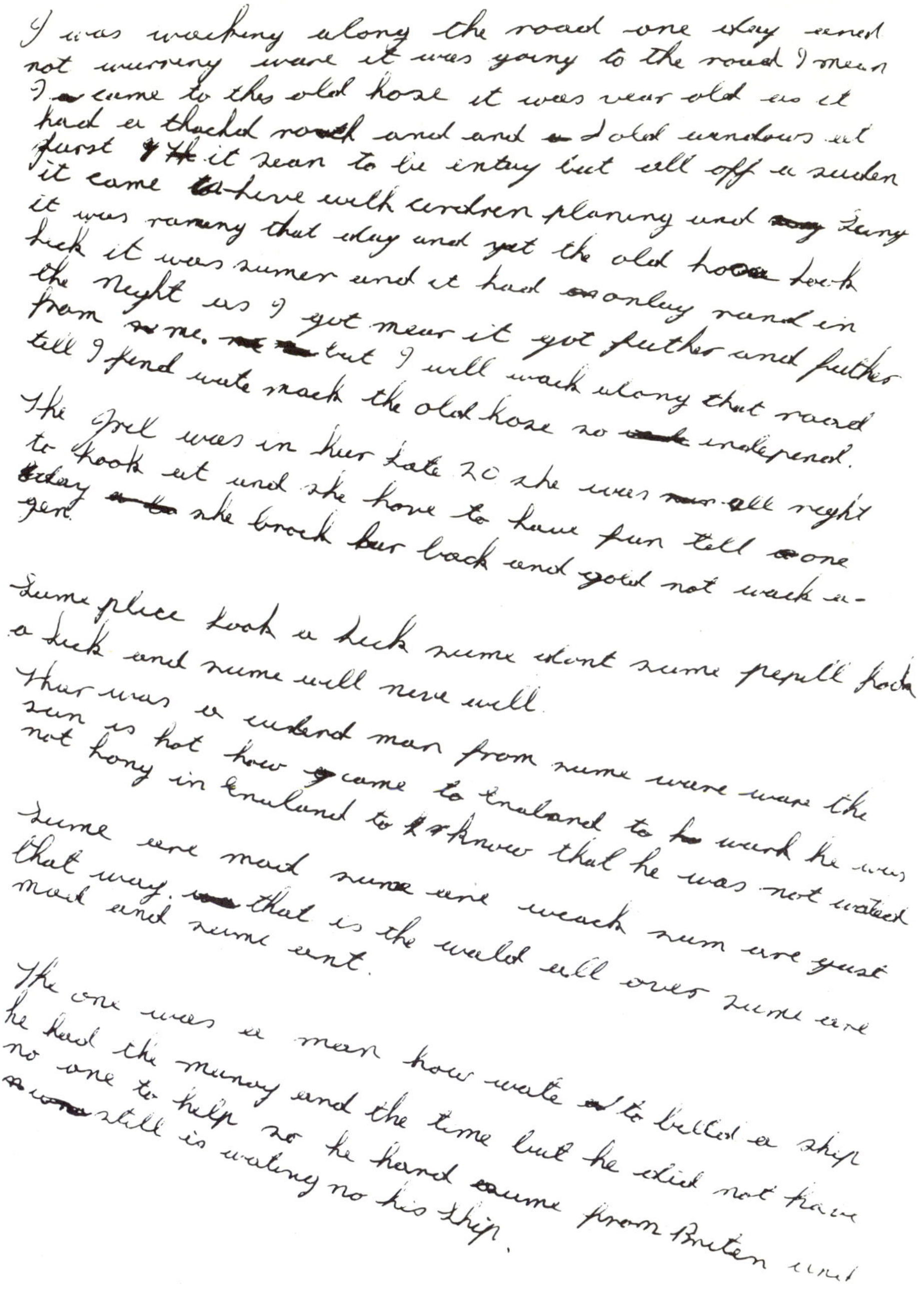

EXAMPLE 2

I want to know *what is wrong with me.*
I feel *depressed most of the time except when I am with a girl.*
I can't *do arithmetic for any length of time.*
I suffer *a lot of loneliness most of the time.*
The happiest time *is when I am away from home.*
The future *I hate to think of the future.*
I need *a girl friend who will take some notice of me.*
My greatest worry is *my mother not my father.*
I am best when *I am with a girl who talks to me.*

I think that the apprehension, the anxiety, and the deepest need for warm adult relationships are clearly shown in these extracts. They are further indications that these young men wanted help, that they were still in a receptive frame of mind and not embittered beyond caring.

Case Study E shows how anxiety produced an auditory hallucinosis.

CASE STUDY E

This young man had a reading age of 9 years and an IQ of 121. He was referred to the SPE by the Army Medical Services after having been referred for hallucinosis and diagnosed as suffering from congenital developmental dyslexia. He gave the characteristic family history of twinning, left-handedness, and ambidexterity with reading difficulties. The Harris test showed a pattern of crossed laterality, and on neurological examination he showed a finger agnosia thus indicating some visuo-spatial disorientation.

E claimed that he first started hearing voices at the age of 9, having heard a buzzing in his ears since he was 6. At first there were several voices that were indistinct, but after a short while they merged and became one voice. This voice was distinct and seemed to come from the left side of his head. He identified the voice as "2109" or "John L. Lennon" and attributed it to the Planet Uranus. He considered that "2109" or "John L. Lennon" was using him to relay messages to other people, namely, top generals in the Pentagon and Kremlin. He thought that the aim of this extraterrestrial being was to bring peace to the world.

When "2109" was not using him for transmission or speaking to him directly, he could hear a continual high-pitched buzzing in his left ear, which he attributed to the transmitter remaining "on net." Apparently the voice had been helpful to him, feeding him answers to questions that otherwise he could not have answered.

E was from a poor, Northern Irish Catholic family. He and his dissimilar twin brother were the youngest of seven siblings. The father abandoned the mother when the twins were still infants. E was left-handed, his twin brother was ambidextrous but very clumsy, and one elder brother was also left-handed as was the maternal grandmother. E states that his childhood was very unhappy—"Because of the voice, I lost all my friends." At school he was backward: "The more I listened to the voice, the worse I did my lessons." In adolescence he tended to be solitary and made very few friends.

He left school at 15 years, worked as a laundry van boy for 5 months, and then worked in a malt factory until the age of 17½ years when he joined the Army. "I joined the Army because I wanted to get away from the mess I had made of my life."

E was described as "a satisfactory soldier" and had qualified as a marksman before attending SPE.

He was placed in the Remedial Centre and subjected to an intense phonic program. He had a typing session daily, and this combined program, together with counseling, enabled him to make rapid progress.

After two or three weeks the hallucinations gradually disappeared, and he showed considerable insight into this. "I think it is all a dream. I must have made it up because I needed security. It was my way of compensating because I wasn't as good as the others."

Examples of his work at the beginning and end of the course are shown in Figures 5.2a and 5.2b.

The anxiety manifest in the preceding case studies is marked also by the psychosomatic preoccupation of 31.25 percent with their own poor health and bodily aches and pains. The majority of men who reported sick did so for what are, medically, very trivial reasons but to them had singular importance. An examination of the medical center records showed that on average every man reported sick at least once during his 10½ week course, for comparatively trivial reasons—headache; pains in the leg, back, or arms; and so forth. It is interesting to note that Coville, Costello, and Rouke (1960) state that low back pains were one of the most commonly stated complaints on sick parade in the U.S. military services during the war. In only a very few cases was any organic cause discovered.

It is, I believe, evident that the neuroses of the men at the SPE were as urgent and complex as the problem of their backwardness. They had to be treated primarily for their neuroses, since the backwardness would not be alleviated until the neuroses responded to therapy.

FIGURE 5.2a. Writing of Case Study E on arrival at the SPE.

```
dearest eileen

            i am glad to hear you are keeping will as it leaves me
the same at present: i have not but in the address as i find it hard to
do so i hope you do not mind! darling i am sorry for thinking you would
think it funey; then i told you i could not read very will;
till your mother & father that i was asking about them and hope thay are
              was
will: eileen i out on the town and i was out with a girl; you see i
could not hilp it for one of my mates was with a girl and she would not
go out with him on till i took her mate out;@@@@@@@@@@@@@
eileen i love you and it will not happen agean;; uei promiss you that;
you are the girl for me will ihave told you about the girl so it is up
to you:
```

An Analysis of the Test Results

At the end of their course the men in the sample were retested on the Cornell Index to establish whether or not any significant changes had occurred in their emotional attitudes. The differences found between the results of the initial and final test scores were tested for significance by "t" test and analysis of variance techniques. The results of the "t" testing are summarized in Appendix E, Table E.3.

Fear and Inadequacy

The first variable subjected to statistical analysis was fear and inadequacy. We have already discussed the importance of this factor to SPE entrants in a learning situation: an overall feeling of inadequacy was the predominant emotional feature coloring their attitudes toward themselves and society. The "t" testing reveals that, for all groups of readers, the levels of fear and inadequacy had fallen to a highly-significant degree over the 10½ week course. An improvement of this magnitude in such a short space of time is a highly satisfactory achievement. The result is interesting in that it shows that even the good readers initially felt themselves to be seriously lacking in personal achievement.

FIGURE 5.2b. Writing of Case Study E at the end of the course.

What I find now is going to be one of the hardest things I have ever said in my life to anyone but I think that there is a time in everyones life when they realise that certain things have to be said or done.

Susan, I find in you a greater security than I have ever found before. I do not mean to impress upon you the problems which I personnally feel.

You have known me for just a short time and I can only ask you to read this letter carefully.

I am a man who has retreated within a wall of his own creation and which no-one else could penetrate.

It all started when my father left home for no apparent reason and being young at the time I blamed myself entirely for what happened between my parents. From that has sprung an insecurity which I have held to this day.

I have been a person who wishes to be on his own and have no relationships with anyone and so formed that invisible wall which kept the friendship and happiness of an ordinary human being away from me. But when I met you I found that you attracted a friendship which I had never experienced in my whole life. In this friendship which grew with time I found that my character formed into that of the individual which I had always wanted to be and which I had so long sought to be.

But then because of my insecurity I began to set up a human barrier between us and subsequently told you lies to make you dislike me. Then I realised rather late that I really did like you and tries to alter the wrong which I had done.

Susan you have been a very understanding girl towards me and I know that I may well have lost your love but your friendship I never hope to lose.

You and your father were the first people ever to penetrate the wall which I had built around myself. I am only sorry that I cannot describe this in more detail.

I have thanked you before for what you have done for me and I hope that you will forgive me for what I have done.

When this result was subjected to an analysis of variance, the findings were as shown in Table 5.18. The analysis indicates that the differences between the mean improvements for the three groups of readers are highly significant. Further analysis reveals that the improvement of the poor readers over the mediocre and good groups is not significant. Since it is the poorest readers who feel their inadequacy most and who make the most significant progress in reading attainment, this result is not unexpected, and the linear component in the analysis is highly significant, indicating that the improvement decreases as the reading age increases.

Depression

Depression is concerned with feelings of dejection and gloom and is often associated with feelings of inadequacy or worthlessness. It is not surprising, therefore, that this figures prominantly in the personality of backward readers and, in particular, among backward adults. The "t" testing for this variable shows that there had been a highly significant improvement in the level of depression for both the poor and mediocre readers; the improvement in level for the good group is significant at 2 percent.

Table 5.19 shows the results of an analysis of variance applied to this factor. The figures indicate that the differences between the mean improvements of the three groups of readers are highly significant. The difference in the improvement of the poor readers over the good is highly significant; that between the poor and mediocre readers is significant at the 1 percent level. No significant difference exists between the improvements of the mediocre and good groups. If one considers the improvements in reading ability achieved by the three groups, it will be seen that the improvement in level of depression becomes less as reading age increases; this is confirmed by the highly significant linear component in the analysis.

Anxiety

Anxiety, the pervasive factor in the life of most of these men, is concerned with feelings of apprehension and alarm for which there does not seem to be any specific basis in reality. The individual tends to be in a continual state of tension and worry. Anxiety is also associated with the emotions in interpersonal relations, and most often indicates a life pattern of insecurity and immaturity. Thus the high level of anxiety among all these reading groups reflected the unfortunate environmental circumstances previously described. It is associated with other nervous reactions and has considerable educational implications, since the

TABLE 5.18. Analysis of Variance Applied to Fear and Inadequacy (Cornell Index)

READING GROUP	N	MEAN	S.D.	DF	P
Poor	31	−4.065	2.265		
Mediocre	104	−2.212	1.973	2	0.0001***
Good	25	−1.960	1.881		

*** Highly significant

TABLE 5.19. Analysis of Variance Applied to Depression (Cornell Index)

READING GROUP	N	MEAN	S.D.	DF	P
Poor	31	−1.000	0.856		
Mediocre	104	−0.587	0.691	2	0.0011***
Good	24	−0.280	0.542		

*** Highly significant

TABLE 5.20. Analysis of Variance Applied to Anxiety (Cornell Index)

READING GROUP	N	MEAN	S.D.	DF	P
Poor	31	−1.322	1.166		
Mediocre	104	−1.269	0.988	2	0.2500
Good	25	−0.920	0.862		

ability to learn or profit by experience is greatly impaired in the very anxious. Thus, if the level of anxiety could be reduced considerably, this would greatly increase the chances of an improvement not only in academic attainment but also in general attitude. Reducing an individual's level of anxiety was, in my opinion, crucial to the whole purpose of the SPE and highlights the vital importance of the father-figure relationship between officer and student. It is, therefore, very gratifying to record that "t" testing shows that in all reading groups there has been a highly significant drop in the level of generalized anxiety. The results of further investigation by an analysis of variance are shown in Table 5.20.

The analysis indicates that the differences in improvement between the three groups of readers are not significant. This result lends support to the hypothesis that anxiety was the overriding characteristic of the men's emotional patterns regardless of academic achievement. It also shows that in this very vital area the overall therapeutic process was just as successful with good readers as with other groups, and refutes earlier implications that perhaps the school was not doing as much as it could, or should, for good readers. This is supported by the lack of significance in either the linear or quadratic components of the analysis.

Neurocirculatory Psychosomatic Symptoms

This variable is associated with such psychosomatic symptoms affecting the circulatory process as palpitations or heavily thumping heart, breathlessness, and heart or chest pains. The results obtained on this subsection of the Cornell Index were somewhat disappointing in view of the very real reductions that were achieved in the general levels of anxiety and inadequacy. The "t" test reveals that the improvement for the good readers is not significant. The improvement of the poor group is significant at the 5 percent level; that of the mediocre is significant at the 1 percent level. The analysis of variance shown in Table 5.21 indicates that there are no significant differences between the improvements of the three groups of readers. The linear component of the analysis is not significant, and the improvement in this case is not proportionate to any increase in reading ability.

Startle Reaction

Startle reactions involve bodily reactions to an emotional pattern of fear, which is closely related to the anxiety syndrome. Since this type of reaction is present to the greatest degree in the poor readers, it is to be expected that this group will show the greatest improvement. The "t" testing shows the poor and mediocre groups both made highly significant improvements; the improvement of the good readers is significant at the 2 percent level. The analysis of variance shown in Table 5.22 shows the differences in improvement between the three groups to be significant at the 1 percent level.

A more detailed analysis shows the difference in improvement of the poor readers over the good to be highly significant; that of the poor over the mediocre readers is not significant. The difference between the improvement of the mediocre over the good readers is significant at the 1 percent level. The linear component of the analysis is highly significant and shows that the level of improvement decreases as reading ability increases.

TABLE 5.21. Analysis of Variance Applied to Neurocirculatory Psychosomatic Symptoms (Cornell Index)

READING GROUP	N	MEAN	S.D.	DF	P
Poor	31	−0.258	0.631		
Mediocre	104	−0.106	0.339	2	0.145
Good	25	−0.080	0.277		

TABLE 5.22. Analysis of Variance Applied to Startle Reactions (Cornell Index)

READING GROUP	N	MEAN	S.D.	DF	P
Poor	31	−1.226	1.055		
Mediocre	104	−0.846	1.012	2	0.0020**
Good	25	−0.280	0.542		

** Significant at the 1 percent level

Psychosomatic Symptoms

We have already stressed the importance of psychosomatic symptoms affecting these men and drawn attention to the high incidence of nervous headaches and bodily aches and pains that had no organic basis. Psychosomatic disorders are usually the result of prolonged or intense emotional stress—they represent the individual's response to some real life situation. The disorders are of a physical nature, but they have a psychological origin and are caused by the frustrating of emotional outlets. In general, psychosomatic disorders are symptomatic of a lack of maturity and responsibility. The "t" testing shows that highly significant reductions in psychosomatic reactions were made by the poor and mediocre readers; the good readers achieved a significant improvement in their condition at the 1 percent level.

The analysis of variance shown in Table 5.23 indicates that the differences between the mean improvements of the three groups of readers are significant at the 5 percent level. Further analysis shows that the difference in improvement between the poor and mediocre readers is not significant; the difference between the poor and good readers is significant at the 5 percent level; and that between the mediocre and good readers is significant at the 2 percent level. The linear component of the analysis is significant at the 1 percent level, and thus there is a tendency toward a smaller reduction in reaction as the reading age increases.

TABLE 5.23. Analysis of Variance Applied to Psychosomatic Symptoms (Cornell Index)

READING GROUP	N	MEAN	S.D.	DF	P
Poor	31	−1.194	1.108		
Mediocre	104	−1.135	1.215	2	0.0427*
Good	25	−0.520	0.872		

* Significant at the 5 percent level

TABLE 5.24. Analysis of Variance Applied to Hypochondriasis-Asthenia (Cornell Index)

READING GROUP	N	MEAN	S.D.	DF	P
Poor	31	−0.387	0.558		
Mediocre	104	−0.202	0.546	2	0.0185*
Good	25	0.000	0.000		

* Significant at the 5 percent level

Hypochondriasis and Asthenia

Persons suffering from hypochondriasis have an over-concern with their health and bodies. Isolated and immature self-centered personalities are especially prone to develop this reaction. Characteristically it is a reaction precipitated by feelings of inadequacy and a lack of fulfillment. It is hardly surprising, therefore, that it is a factor found in all reading groups and to a much greater degree among the poor readers.

Asthenia is principally identified as a reaction to unhappy and frustrating life experiences and circumstances. In its common and milder form it produces somatic complaints, listlessness, and a general lack of interest in life. The reaction is characterized by headaches, backaches, dizzy spells, and indigestion; the individual habitually complains of being tired and lacking in energy. The educational implications are summarized by Burt (1955), who states that the asthenic "may remain for ever at a standstill whenever work requires a retentive memory." Any improvement of this condition would, therefore, be of considerable value to the whole therapeutic process. The "t" testing shows the improvements of the poor and mediocre groups to be significant. The good readers show no improvement whatsoever, the means from the initial and final testing being equal. This is slightly surprising as, although the incidence of this reaction among the good readers is less than half that among the poor, it is only fractionally less than the incidence among the mediocre group who made highly significant progress. However, the linear component of the analysis of variance shown in Table 5.24 is significant and shows that any improvement in this condition decreases as reading ability increases.

The differences in improvement between the three reading groups are found to be significant at the 5 percent level. Further analysis reveals that the improvement of the poor readers is significantly greater than that of the good at the 1 percent level; the differences in improvement between the poor and mediocre, and the mediocre and good readers, are not significant.

Gastrointestinal Psychosomatic Symptoms

These reactions are expressions of anxiety involving the gastrointestinal system; a major component is an excessive and unresolved dependency problem. Quite often attacks are precipitated by sudden intense emotional reactions. The incidence among the poor and mediocre readers is nearly twice that among the good, and this is not surprising. The results of an analysis of this variable are surprising, however. The improvement of the poor group is significant at the 1 percent level, but the improvement of the mediocre readers is highly significant. The analysis of variance shown in Table 5.25 shows the differences between the mean improvements of the three groups to be significant at the 5 percent level.

Further analysis shows that the differences in improvements between the poor and mediocre groups, and the poor and good, are not significant; the difference between the improvement of the mediocre and good readers is significant at the 1 percent level. The quadratic component of the analysis is significant, thus confirming the findings of the "t" test that the mediocre readers have made the greatest improvement. There does not appear to be any logical explanation for this.

Sensitivity and Suspiciousness

Men who have suffered unfavorable environmental conditions, and whose life patterns reflect a history of failure and frustration, will frequently tend to be excessively sensitive and suspicious in their social and personal adjustments. They believe that people usually misunderstand them, that they have been, and still are, picked on, and that they have not been treated fairly. Surprisingly these feelings were greatest among the mediocre readers, and there is also a high incidence among the poor group. The "t" testing shows that there was a highly significant improvement in these conditions for all groups of readers. The analysis of variance shown in Table 5.26 shows the differences in the mean im-

TABLE 5.25. Analysis of Variance Applied to Gastrointestinal Psychosomatic Symptoms (Cornell Index)

READING GROUP	N	MEAN	S.D.	DF	P
Poor	31	−0.452	0.850		
Mediocre	104	−0.529	0.780	2	0.0297*
Good	25	−0.080	0.277		

* Significant at the 5 percent level

TABLE 5.26. Analysis of Variance Applied to Sensitivity and Suspicion (Cornell Index)

READING GROUP	N	MEAN	S.D.	DF	P
Poor	31	−0.806	0.703		
Mediocre	104	−1.221	1.004	2	0.0097**
Good	25	−0.680	0.852		

** Significant at the 1 percent level

TABLE 5.27. Analysis of Variance Applied to Troublesome Psychopathy (Cornell Index)

READING GROUP	N	MEAN	S.D.	DF	P
Poor	31	−0.806	1.327		
Mediocre	104	−0.538	0.812	2	0.1821
Good	25	−0.360	0.757		

TABLE 5.28. Analysis of Variance Applied to Total Score on Cornell Index

READING GROUP	N	MEAN	S.D.	DF	P
Poor	31	−11.516	7.767		
Mediocre	104	−8.644	7.070	2	0.0044**
Good	25	−5.160	5.535		

** Significant at the 1 percent level

provements of the three reading groups to be significant at the 1 percent level.

Further analysis shows that there is no significant difference between the improvements of the poor and good readers, and the poor and medium groups. The difference in the improvement of the medium over the good readers is significant at the 1 percent level. In this analysis the quadratic component is highly significant, and again the mediocre readers have registered the greatest improvement—a logical result, since this variable was present to a much greater degree in this group.

Troublesome Psychopathy

Under this heading we find that the Cornell Index reveals the antisocial reactions symptomatic of emotional immaturity: poor judgment, poor sense of responsibility, and an inability to appreciate the consequences of one's behavior. Its findings concerning individuals who have been at odds with society reflect the history of previous delinquent acts discussed earlier. This reaction is also associated with homes that are lacking in emotional warmth and in which the individual feels rejected; once again this reinforces our earlier findings about the impact that unsatisfactory environmental conditions make upon the individual. As expected, the mean scores of the poor and mediocre groups are much greater than the scores of the good readers.

Application of "t" tests shows that the overall improvement of the poor readers is significant at the 1 percent level, that of the good readers is significant at the 5 percent level, and the improvement of the mediocre group is highly significant. The results of an analysis of variance are shown in Table 5.27. The analysis reveals that there are no significant differences between the mean improvements of the three reading groups.

Total Cornell Index Score

The improvements made in the various subsections of the Cornell Index are reflected in the overall scores. The "t" tests show that over the whole test range highly significant improvements in "personal" emotions and attitudes were recorded by all the reading groups. The analysis of variance results for the total scores are shown in Table 5.28.

The differences between the mean improvements of the three groups of readers are significant at the 1 percent level. Further analysis shows the difference in improvement of the poor and mediocre readers over the good group to be significant at the 5 percent level; that of the poor readers over the good is highly significant. The linear component of the analysis is highly significant and shows the overall improvement decreasing as the reading age increases.

Summary

The analysis of the screening confirms the subjective impression that on arrival at the SPE these men were suffering from emotional reactions arising from inadequacy, anxiety, and a lack of fulfillment. Many had unstable home environments. Generally they were apprehensive about what was going to happen to them. The Cornell Index scores portray a negative self-image that is perhaps a hallmark of their upbringing. We find a marked introversion; a greater than average preoccupation with psychosomatic symptoms. There is a recurrent pattern of generalized anxiety, and the men can be described as emotionally immature.

The analysis shows that with sympathetic and understanding remedial care, based upon an accurate assessment and diagnosis of their overall needs, remarkable improvements were effected in those "personal" emotions and adjustments that have such close association with academic success and failure. The general levels of maturity and confidence were raised, and the Army can claim to have succeeded as an instrument of socialization where the home had failed. The development of more mature emotional responses through a program of individual attention and encouragement helped these men find what Bradshaw (1953) referred to as a "place in the sun," which they might otherwise never have attained. Understandably this new-found confidence is reflected in their increased attainments in the SPE and PSO test batteries.

Confirmation of the extent of their overall adjustment and improved status is provided by three studies undertaken by the Institute of Army Education. The studies compared wastage and survival rates of equal numbers of ex-SPE and non-SPE recruits who were matched as far as possible for ability and training unit or origin. The results are set out in Table 5.29.

The differences in the survival rates are highly significant, and these show the ex-SPE recruit to have a more stable and positive attitude toward continued Service employment—part of a general adjustment he has made to life.

The significant improvements achieved in emotional adjustment give added emphasis to the point made earlier that these men, despite their previous educational and social handicaps, do earnestly desire to improve their all-round standards and status in life.

TABLE 5.29. Survival Rates of Ex-SPE Students and Comparative Groups

YEAR RECRUITED	SURVIVAL RATES	
	EX-SPE RECRUITS (PERCENTAGE)	COMPARATIVE GROUP (PERCENTAGE)
1963	36.6	13.7
1967	52.3	45.5
1968	53.2	36.2

The analysis of the results of the Cornell Index appears to dispel any implications that the school was somehow failing to motivate the best readers. It shows, too, that even they have "personal" problems that, unless alleviated, are likely to inhibit not only their present performance but also their future training potential.

CONCLUSIONS

The analyses of levels of performance on attainment tests before and after the SPE course clearly show that, despite their deprived environmental circumstances and social maladjustment, these men in the space of 10½ weeks made measurable and meaningful progress in the basic skills.

A comparison of the progress made by the three groups of readers shows a strange map of improvement—strange because it is far from uniform. Contrary to what might be expected, it is often those with the lowest initial standards of performance who make the most significant progress.

The study also shows that lack of previous academic success is no indication of a lack of innate ability. The analyses of the performance of the three groups on the Personnel Tests administered before and after the SPE course confirm the all-round improvement registered on the SPE Battery. A large percentage of men improved their overall selection grade, which in many cases made them eligible for more technical training. Their potential as soldiers was thus considerably increased.

The results of the limited ophthalmic investigation in conjunction with the Bath Eye Infirmary show that a clear relationship exists between eye disorders, cross laterality, and poor performance in reading.

The analysis of the results obtained on the Cornell Index vindicates the approach to education practiced at the SPE: the education of the whole is of far greater importance than any statistical improvement in academic attainment. It would appear from the results of this analysis that the most relevant part of the training was the opportunity for free and creative activities designed to relieve inner tensions and conflicts. This overall improvement in self-esteem, modified attitudes, and sense of responsibility is confirmed by three studies undertaken by the Institute of Army Education. These studies were to ascertain comparative waste of soldiers who did and did not attend SPE courses in 1963, 1967, and 1968. In all groups there was a significantly greater survival rate for the ex-SPE student.

The findings of this study, therefore, are that the training program at the SPE was successful not only in human terms but probably also as a more far-reaching financial and recruitment investment.

6 A Specific Remedial Program

You have got very badly to want to get rid of the old before something new will appear.

D. H. LAWRENCE

At this point I want to look specifically at a particular remedial program that was carried out in the Remedial Centre from 1964 to 1969 under what were, as far as possible, controlled conditions. It must be realized, however, that in a military unit with a training program organized for staggered intakes and very conscious of cost-effectiveness requirements, true experimental conditions in the psychological sense are not readily achieved.

As has been explained earlier, we took a most unpromising group of students in the bottom 10 percent of the school population (i.e., those with a Reading Age of 8 years or less) and attempted one specific scheme of educational therapy. Conducted on a small scale, the experiment was a straightforward attempt to compare results. Although every effort was made to obviate the Hawthorne effect, it is possible that some aspect of this may be an underlying factor in the results obtained. Despite this, the striking results are worth emphasizing; they will have much meaning to others working in this field.

NEED FOR A NEW APPROACH TO READING

The students chosen for this experimental program comprised the despondent cases of reading failure who, judging from previous experience, would not make sufficient progress during a 10½ week course to enable them to acquire the communication skills needed in daily life. An improvement of some 3–6 months in reading age does not create any significant change in literacy standards. This was therefore a matter of some concern, and it was evident that we had to find a new approach—an approach that was not immediately inhibited by the psychological barrier of reactivated feelings of failure, frustration, and mistrust.

"If I couldn't do no good with them letters in ten years of bleeding school I ain't going to do nothing in ten !!!!!!!!!!! weeks." This was a frequent and typical reaction from men who had failed in reading and who, furthermore, were well aware that they had failed. Thus the greatest problem was anxiety, which had been created by a fear of failure and which was paralyzing their motivation and creating emotional attitudes hostile to any remedial techniques.

Struggling with these particularly backward groups, I became convinced, after much careful individual diagnosis, that while environmental factors and ineffective teaching methods might initially have been responsible for the retarded state of the students concerned, these factors were now of secondary importance. The extent of their backwardness, coupled with a history of failure and frustration, had created a significant psychological barrier in these students since in our approach to reading we were not offering anything that appeared new to them. Further investigations led me to the conclusion, supported by Downing and Gardner (1962) in their research into remedial work with children, that the phonic inconsistency of traditional orthography (TO) presented a recurring stumbling block; furthermore, this inconsistency—and the confusion it created—had considerable adverse effect on the motivation of these men.

The spelling pattern of our traditional orthography can fail the slow learner both visually and aurally; therefore, it can produce confusion no matter which major teaching method is used. The look-and-say method depends upon association between the visual pattern of a word and the actual meaning of that word. However, the student finds that he may very well be faced with a great variety of patterns for the same word, as shown in Figure 6.1.

The phonic method of teaching reading requires a relationship between the printed word and the word symbol when spoken, thus enabling a student to read by building up a whole word from the individual sounds of letters or syllables. Unfortunately, in our traditional spelling he is faced with the fact that one sound may be presented in many different ways (e.g., though, owe, hoe, show, no, sew, coal, yeoman, yolk) and one letter may convey many differing sounds (e.g., bone, gone, done, one) as shown in Figure 6.2.

What these backward readers urgently required, therefore, was a

FIGURE 6.1. Visual patterns of selected words in traditional orthography and i.t.a.

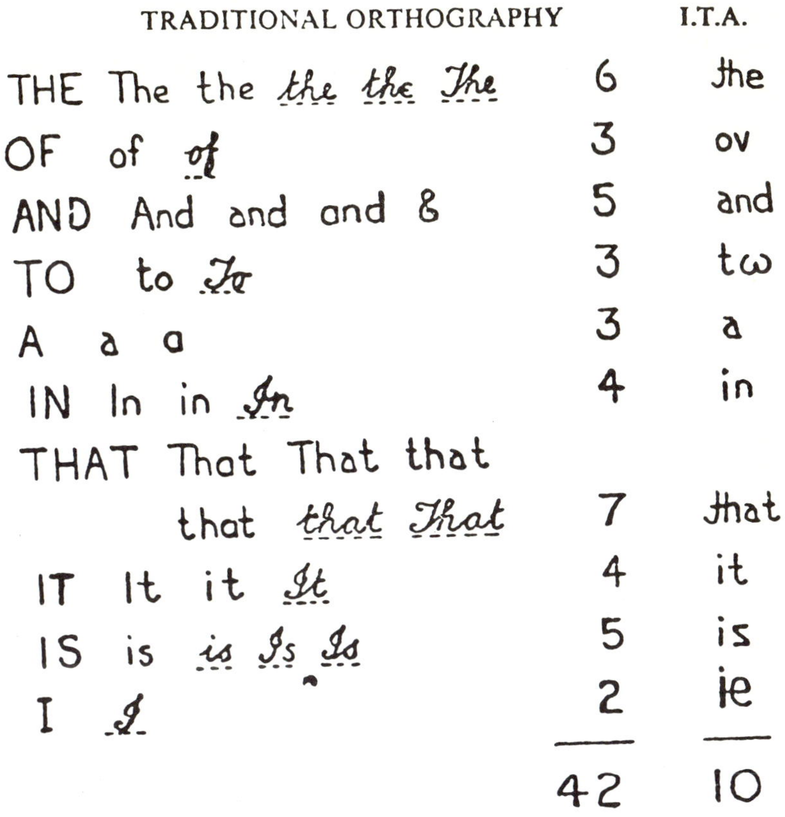

completely new approach to their difficulties—a simplification of sound symbols that remained constant regardless of prefix or suffix. An investigation of the commercial teaching aids available, and brief and unsuccessful experimentation with some of these schemes, led to an investigation of the possibilities of Sir James Pitman's initial teaching alphabet (i.t.a.).

SELECTION OF i.t.a. AS A TEACHING MEDIUM

The constructional principles of i.t.a. are now well publicized and understood. Although this was primarily designed as an aid to reading

FIGURE 6.2. Different ways one sound may be presented in traditional orthography compared to i.t.a.

TRADITIONAL ORTHOGRAPHY	I.T.A.
I, height, eye,	
child, file, lie,	
sign, high, island,	ie
guide, buy, by,	
dye, aisle, choir.	

in the initial stages, it appeared that i.t.a. might well meet our requirements and greatly reduce the difficulties encountered by these men for the following reasons:

1. It has a complete stability of visual pattern; that is, it is wholly lower case.
2. It depends upon the simplest form of sound/symbol relations.
3. It makes possible an appreciable reduction in alternative spellings for the basic sounds of the English language.

In addition, for despondent students who have experienced reading failure, it has a distinct psychological advantage in that, while retaining certain familiar symbols from TO, it is different enough to be new and not associated with their previous failure. There was no dearth of experimental material concerning the use of this new learning me-

FIGURE 6.3. The initial teaching alphabet.

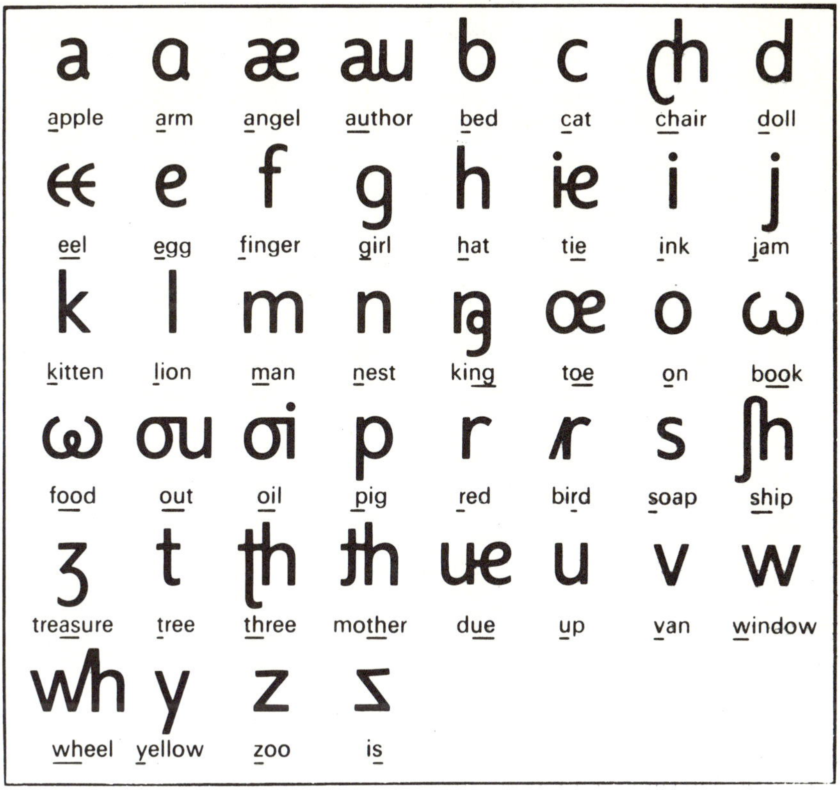

dium with children, but no one at that time had attempted to use it as a remedial tool with adults. Despite all the widely published claims then being made for the new medium, we were disturbed by the possibility that attempting something entirely new might be a source of much more concern for adults than for children. The following statement by Mazurkiewicz (1966) is typical of the viewpoint of the protagonists: "i.t.a. epitomizes a psychologically valid principle followed in other areas of life; that learning proceeds from the simple to the complex." It was vital that our approach should be as scientific as possible, and also somewhat cautious. It was decided, therefore, to mount a controlled program to investigate the potential of i.t.a. as a remedial reading medium for adults.

The initial teaching alphabet is shown in Figure 6.3. I have often been asked why for those having difficulty in decoding an alphabet containing only 26 symbols, the decision was taken to experiment with one that uses 44. This whole question was, of course, discussed fully before deciding to undertake the experiment. Although it is true that in i.t.a. there are 44 characters, in TO, because of its many variants, upper-case and cursive characterizations, supplemented by many digraphs, there are in fact more than 2,000 different sound representations to be learned. With i.t.a. the learner-reader has, therefore, far fewer characters to learn and remember.

In our discussion we also noted that i.t.a. removed the uncertainty and confusion of spatial order in reading, since the pronunciation always follows the normal reading direction. This was a factor of considerable importance since it was an area where our most backward readers found many difficulties and much uncertainty. Consequently, we decided that the inherent stability of visual pattern and sound/symbol relationships, plus the factor that they had never failed with this medium, far outweighed any risks that might be involved.

In considering this the following factors were also recognized:

1. The majority of students were already familiar with 24 of the 44 characters (i.e., those retained from the Roman alphabet), even though they were unable to utilize them effectively.
2. In their own writing the men adopted a phonic style of spelling greatly akin to i.t.a., as shown in the following extract from a soldier's letter home: "wun dae ie went insied a hous to get sum wauter the lady gave me sum tee."

This example also shows how those who write in this fashion might well be expected to benefit considerably from the spatial certainty of i.t.a.

Objectives

The aims of the program were to find, if possible, answers to the following questions:

1. Was it practicable to use i.t.a. as a remedy for disability in reading and reading failure in adults?
2. If this medium proved successful as a therapeutic measure, would the slow-learning adult then be able to effect the transfer to reading effectively in TO?
3. What effect, if any, would the use of the medium have on the overall attitudes and on the reading habits of retarded adults?

It was decided that these questions could best be answered by the use of matched pairs in a tightly controlled program.

THE MATCHING PROCESS

The criteria used in the matching process were the initial scores in the following tests: (1) Compound Series Test (nonverbal IQ), (2) The Holborn Reading Scale, and (3) The Holborn Comprehension Test. In addition, all students were assessed on individual performance on the following diagnostic reading tests by Schonell: (1) Test of Directional Attack on Words, R.6, and (2) Visual Word Discrimination Test, R.7. Spelling was tested by means of the SPE Spelling Test, which consisted of recognition of incorrect spellings and recall of the correct ones. (Refer to Appendix D for a description of the tests used.)

The pairs, of which there were ultimately 50, were arranged so that the differences in reading age were not greater than 3 months. On all other tests the score differences were not to be greater than 5 points. Details of the scores obtained are set out in Appendix H, Tables H.1 and H.2.

No man was ever forced to use i.t.a. as a learning medium. All those concerned were consulted, and i.t.a. was explained to them. They also received an outline of their remedial program and were given the opportunity of rejecting it. During the 5 years in which I used the medium no student ever declined to participate. The general reaction is best summed up by this soldier's remarks: "I'll try anything once and I couldn't be no worse than I am now, could I? All I want is to bleeding read. You can't do nothing if you can't ——— read!"

In the early stages of our program we confined our attention to the improvement of reading because of the limitations imposed by time and the distaste for, and fear of, writing among the men.

UNIFORMITY OF INSTRUCTION

A criticism of some of the earlier i.t.a. experiments, both in America and in England, is that insufficient attention was paid to controlled situations so that one could not be absolutely sure that the improvements obtained were due solely to the i.t.a. factor. However, it is one thing to criticize but another to really overcome the difficulties involved.

In a military training establishment, staff and time are ever in short supply. It was not possible either to draft an additional instructor to the

Remedial Centre to assist with this experimental program or to allocate any further time to the educational content of the students' course. Under the circumstances, therefore, the only way to experiment was for all the students to be taught by me. This, of course, limited the number of students who could be matched and taught over exactly the same period of time. However, it did have the advantage of obviating as far as possible differences that might have arisen from instructor attitudes, enthusiasms, competition, and so forth. The total of the combined groups was restricted to six students at any one time. In addition, both groups were taught on an individual and group basis in the same large Remedial Centre room, thus experiencing the same general atmosphere. This had the added advantage that both groups were together for informal discussion, daily news items, job introduction, and remedial therapy on group and individual problems.

One serious concern was the type of reading material available in i.t.a. All commercially produced readers were designed for use by very young children in the initial stages of reading; unlike Sir James Pitman, we felt these were highly unsuitable for adults and would only create further antagonism toward the learning situation. We thus transliterated our own highly exciting (we thought) stories based on war heroes, battles, and so forth, using a typewriter kindly loaned by the i.t.a. Foundation. An example of this material is shown in Figure 6.4.

Regimental Orders, "What's on?" notices, and similar material were all transliterated and placed in the Remedial Centre along with their TO counterparts. In this way we were able to exercise the greatest care in ensuring that both the experimental and the control groups were also able to use a Rank Language Master. A Language Master is a machine that acts as a dual track tape recorder, but instead of the conventional reels of tape, it uses cards with a strip of dual track magnetic tape along the base. The cards may display letters, words, and appropriate illustrations, which are linked to the master track recording. Blank cards are also available for those wishing to produce a specially structured vocabulary. The card is fed into the machine and passes from right to left; this way, the words and sounds imprinted on the left side become visible and audible first, thus reinforcing the correct reading direction of left to right. The student is able not only to hear the recorded text but also to make his own recording, play this back, and thus compare it with the master tape. These procedures may be repeated as often as he wishes. The machine is compact, light in weight, and the operating process is very simple since controls have been reduced to a minimum. Headphones are available so that the machine may be used without disturbing other students in the same room. A program for the Rank Lan-

FIGURE 6.4. Excerpt from "Storiz ov Wurld Waur 2" produced at the SPE in i.t.a.

battl in ŧhe deseɼt
****

rommel woz ŧhe jeneral œveɼ ŧhe jeɼman army in ŧhe deseɼt and hɛɛ had led hiz army tω victory af-teɼ victory œveɼ ŧhe britiʃh army.

ɛɛꞓh dæ ŧhe larj jeɼman tanks wωd attack. ɷr tanks weɼ smaulleɼ and cωd not matꞓh ŧhe poweɼ and spɛɛd ov ŧhe jeɼman mark v tank. wɛɛ had fueeɼ gunz, a smaulleɼ army and wɛɛ cωd not win agænst suꞓh oddz.

ŧhe men in ɷr army weɼ bræv but ŧhæ nɛɛded mor ŧhan brævery tω win battlz. ŧhæ nɛɛded gunz, tanks and ʃhellz.

in 1942 ie woz a sœldieɼ in ŧhe dezeɼt waur in norŧh africa. wɛɛ had bɛɛn pωʃht back up tω nɷ but ŧhe tiem had cum for us tω fiet back and fiet back hard.

wɛɛ weɼ sent mor armz and a nue

guage Master was devised in both TO and i.t.a. based upon a soldier's "need to know" vocabulary with illustrations related to his military training and environment. Every soldier in each group was allocated a period of 15 minutes daily on a machine.

When typewriters were introduced as an additional learning aid, each group had one electric typewriter (IBM Selectric) and one manual typewriter as basic equipment. The i.t.a. group also had one manual TO machine for use during and after the period of transition.

Although we adapted our methods to meet the needs of each individual, the same general procedure was followed. In both groups the first step was to use whatever knowledge they possessed in an attempt to achieve some early success and thus maintain motivation. The students were introduced to long and short vowel sounds by means of letter cards and flash cards. Reinforcement was provided by a tactile and kinesthetic approach, the aim being that at the end of the first intensive session the student should be able to put together letters that produced a word of one syllable. The combination of audio-visual stimuli used on the Rank Language Master proved to be a valuable aid at this stage and evoked favorable responses from both groups of students. They felt the benefits immediately, since the programs were devised to build key words and phrases for a basic personal and military vocabulary, and also for daily practice in analysis, synthesis, and aural and visual discrimination. An interesting side effect from the use of these machines was that many men in both groups improved the clarity of their diction. This we attributed to the simple but effective inbuilt facility that this machine possesses for self-correction. The TO programs written for the apparatus were also used as a reinforcement aid when consolidating during the period of transition from i.t.a.

When the students had acquired the ability to build words consisting of two or three sounds, they went straight on to basic reading books, the Downing Readers, the American "Easy to Read" program, and SPE-produced materials.

Throughout the programs each student each day received two intensive individual sessions of oral phonic practice with the instructor. These sessions lasted 15 minutes and included analysis, synthesis, and discriminations. Every student also had a morning and afternoon session of 15 minutes in which to read aloud to the instructor and discuss progress and difficulties. In the early stages when the men had not reached the reading stage this was used for word-building exercises. The students also played word games like "Snap," "Lexicon," "Scrabble," and crosswords. I adapted the TO game materials to i.t.a. During the whole program the progress of each man was logged by means of frequent edited tape recordings, which many of the men ultimately came to regard as a great source of amusement and enjoyment. In a period of relaxation later in a student's course a frequent plea was, "Please, Sir, may I hear how bad I was?" This attitude, however, served a most useful purpose in giving hope and encouragement to anxious and apprehensive newcomers to the remedial section.

When the typewriter was introduced into the remedial program, each man had a 30-minute daily session in the mornings for free writing and a further session for controlled vocabulary and comprehension exercises each afternoon. Duplicate copies of all work were filed to help monitor progress.

During the program the men did, of course, attend all the normal military training activities such as drill, P.T., and games. In the time devoted to educational studies, the day was divided into rhythmic bursts of intense activity followed by sessions of relaxation with games (such as Scrabble and Lexicon) and general discussion.

STAGE I OF THE EXPERIMENT

The first few weeks of our program revealed one very important finding. This concerned the level of material acceptable to this type of man. We had always assumed that these men would require exciting reading matter connected with war heroes, space travel, science fiction, and so on; as has been illustrated in Figure 6.4 we produced our own material. We were somewhat surprised to discover that those making rapid progress with i.t.a. enjoyed any reading matter they were able to master. It appeared that what is vitally important in the early stages is not the content but a man's pleasure in his ability to turn a page having mastered the story so far. It is the feeling of confidence and competence in handling the written symbol. In the early stages he is sufficiently satisfied and motivated by success in reading and understanding, so that no matter how apparently trivial the content, he is willing to practice his new-found ability. Perhaps this enjoyment of the simplest stories is yet further proof of early cultural deprivation; particularly that deprivation of language experience at an early age when someone should have been reading to him. It is interesting to note, however, that members of the control group making slower and more laborious progress with TO did not show the same voracious appetite for reading material.

When the first students had achieved complete fluency in i.t.a. by the end of the first six weeks, we approached with some anxiety that *bête noire* of i.t.a., the period of transition. At that particular time critics of the alphabet were vociferous in expressing grave doubts about the ability of children to overcome the difficulty of transition. Charges and countercharges concerning this had been made in numerous letters to the press, and the issue unfortunately had become highly charged emotionally. Hence our considerable apprehension at that particular point in our program. We had held long discussions with the commandant and the chief instructor on how this assumed barrier could best be overcome. In fact the situation was taken out of our hands and resolved, perhaps fortuitously, by the most advanced student.

One morning I was called away from the reading group with which I was working to discuss an important medical problem concerning one of the students. On rejoining the group I was informed by a soldier whose face was covered in smiles of almost unbelievable satisfaction that "'ere Sir, I read two pages of this while you was in there!" He then turned to his companion and said in a loud triumphant voice, "Look, I've done it! I can ——— well read proper books!"

In my absence he had taken a book from the cupboard and started to read it. This unexpected episode set the pattern for the future. Our experience was that not only was the transition achieved without any difficulty and with little or no regression but the students made the transfer in their own time when they felt themselves to be ready for the change—it appeared to be an almost unconscious act. In addition, the backward adult, as opposed to the infant learner, is unconsciously making the transition in his daily routine. While the remedial study room was placarded with cartoons with i.t.a. captions, "What's on" notices, Part I Daily Orders reproduced in i.t.a., they did see TO newspapers, magazines, letters from home, cinema billboards, and so forth, so that they were, in fact, reading and improving in traditional orthography all the time that they were acquiring confidence and fluency in i.t.a.

After some 15 months it had become clear that i.t.a. had a very important part to play in alleviating the reading retardation of this type of adult. In a report to the Directorate of Army Education, we were able to include the following statement:

> A substantial contribution to its effectiveness is undoubtedly the early success rate which is achieved. We have no hesitation in claiming that results have been quite remarkable, far exceeding anything hitherto achieved at the School by conventional remedial methods.

The following case histories illustrate some of the astonishing progress that was made. Test scores for these two cases are included in Table H.1 (Appendix H).

CASE F

A soldier aged 35, F had an initial reading age of 6 years. As an evacuee, he had been brought up in the Canadian Outback, where there was no school and where he had also been completely deprived of a cultural background. Having returned to England at the age of 13 as a noneffective reader, he was placed at the back of the class and left to his own devices. On arrival at the SPE he was unable to read the simplest sentence without painful hesitation and repetition. After 36 hours instruction in i.t.a., he was able to read an i.t.a. textbook, including dialogue, in an easy and relaxed manner with all the correct expression and emphasis.

He was retained at SPE after the 12-week course and gained his Army Certificate in Education, Third Class, with ease, producing a page of free writing with only two spelling errors. His reading age when he left was 13, an increase of 7 years! His mechanical and problem arithmetic scores had also increased by 3⅔ years and 2 years, respectively. This man's IQ was around 85.

CASE G

A soldier aged 26, G was unable to cope with the simplest of our preliminary readers when he joined the remedial class. He too was able to read an i.t.a. text with ease and fluency after some 30 hours instruction. By the end of his course he had attained a reading age of 9 years 9 months. His mechanical and problem arithmetic scores had increased by 1⅔ and 2½ years, respectively.

This man is of particular interest in that initially he was extremely resentful and suspicious of attempts to help him. He had "tried it all before so what's the point of bothering." He suffered considerable emotional problems because of the unsympathetic attitude of his family. He never went home on weekend leave because, as he put it, "of the mickey taking." Success in reading completely changed his outlook; he cut his smoking down from over 50 to 5 cigarettes a day, and by the end of the course went home every weekend because he no longer felt inferior and unwanted. He described i.t.a. as the finest thing that had happened to him in his whole life. He had found the whipping boy upon whom he could unload the failures of his past: "I'm all right, it's the teachers and alphabet that were wrong!"

Results

Stage I of our experiment was concluded after 25 pairs had completed their course. At this stage the differences in improvement between the two groups of readers were subjected to statistical analysis. The analysis showed the improvement of the i.t.a. group to be highly significant in all the tests; the improvements of the TO group were not significant. This significant disparity between the improvements of the two groups had become apparent early in the experiment. The mean improvement in reading age of the i.t.a. group was 23 months compared with 6 months for the control group. This improvement also compared favorably with the mean improvement in reading age of 15 months for the whole school (thus including those readers classified as mediocre and good).

While it had been evident that the i.t.a. group was making more progress in reading attainment, the all-round superiority in improvement of this group was somewhat surprising. Since in the early stages of the experiment, we had concentrated on reading, we had not expected any real and direct impact on writing and spelling. In any event, one would not expect i.t.a. to have much, if any, effect on the vagaries of TO spelling. Nevertheless, the improvement of the experimentals in these skills was well up to the school mean. The reason was undoubtedly the broadening of their vocabulary and language concepts as a result of their increased powers of communication. The most unexpected carry-over of ability, however, was in arithmetic. The groups had concentrated entirely on reading, yet the arithmetical skills of the i.t.a. readers had improved proportionately. This carry-over was to be expected in problem arithmetic where reading attainment has a direct bearing on the comprehension required to achieve a correct solution, but it was remarkable that the same improvement should also be evident in mechanical arithmetic, concerned only with numerical calculations. We suspected that these results might well have occurred because the first experimentals had felt that they were being privileged by some special type of treatment; we therefore decided to see whether or not this pattern of all-round superiority of improvement would continue.

However, the highly significant gains of the i.t.a. group in reading ability and comprehension were not the most impressive aspect of the experiment so far. By far the most important achievement was in the general outlook and attitude of the i.t.a. students, in their new-found confidence and increased self-respect. This confidence in their own ability to achieve success had a marked effect upon their reactions, not only to academic progress but also to each other. They became far more cooperative and less antisocial. This is something that is not conveyed by statistics but is dramatically evident from the library of tape recordings. The confident and relaxed approach, the improvements in expression and phrasing, and the removal of tensions are self-evident and in marked contrast to the still halting, worried approach of the control group. This factor, more than any statistics of increased technical ability, led to the establishing of i.t.a. as a remedial medium at the school and led also to the next stage in our experiment.

STAGE II OF THE EXPERIMENT

On my visits to the United States I had the good fortune to have many discussions with that noted American scholar, Ben D. Wood. In 1932 Wood and F. Freeman had made a notable experimental study of the use of typewriters as a learning aid for children. They suggested first that teaching a child to write longhand not only is unnecessary but may greatly restrict his rate of achievement. We decided, therefore, to investigate the possible uses of the typewriter as a remedial tool to aid the communication of thoughts, ideas, and emotions through the printed word. The distaste that the backward adult has for the complex tasks of writing has been previously mentioned. Not only is the learner faced with recalling each letter in a fixed and frequently illogical order, but also he requires draftsmanship for the actual reproduction. It seemed that the typewriter might well aid the identification, comparison, and selection of shapes since these are ever present on the keyboard. In addition, the required shape could be clearly reproduced simply by depressing a key. This is particularly so in the case of electric typewriters where everything, apart from the insertion of paper, is a matter of touching a key; the greatest advantage is that the clarity of reproduction is quite unaffected by finger pressure.

There were other important factors to be considered regarding typewriters and these backward adults. The typewriter was to the majority a symbol of that white collar world to which they aspired but had never been able to gain access. Also, many of the men had girl friends or sisters who worked with such machines. Here then was an opportunity to use machines from that hitherto unattainable world and a means of acquiring a different status in their own eyes, as well as greater respect from friends and relations.

In this second stage of our experiment we were greatly indebted to the Army Ordnance Services for the provision of standard manual typewriters, and to the Educational Services of IBM, which kindly loaned two Selective typewriters (an i.t.a. machine and a TO machine).

The Reading Program continued as before, with the exception that every soldier in each group was given at least one hour daily on an electric typewriter. The effect of the i.t.a. Selectric machine was startling and appeared to release all the urge for communication that had been dammed up in these men for so long. Many were able to communicate with family and friends in an acceptable and legible form for the first time in their lives. The letter illustrated in Figure 6.5a was produced by a young soldier in 1½ hours on the first occasion that he had ever used a typewriter in his life.

FIGURE 6.5a. Letter produced by soldier in 1½ hours the first time he had used a typewriter.

daer john & all,
i hope you arc all kepping will, and firt.
i hope at you enhugnx your holudag, on the 4, julg, i wen home
and i,wen hap to your house do you are no your holidag your muther
sed at you am finished your mortor, bycle iforth you wooth ar tining
your mortor, bycle lis you on your holudag,
by the lah i go camping and climblng cn the 31, julg, tin we as
a*** 5, dag lenyf hanther at we that onlg a forniyht to dou at
the scool win i go to beyk to baskpool at lanth, o by the loh i
hat ben to venth and see ant het me to go ayihn in sepe,
i hat a gorth time so i will go ayihn in sepe hat fiat heat,
i am going to palth football to dag in thed of judo it is a
gehit htir pal pethes firsh wundag and i molih don judo bot i am
not don in it is wenk, wen we go camping we dou climbing and canoeing
and allso sinlaing it sedlh be forth bot it is onli of 4, dag,
bol the is a conislaing for 5, dag, lenyf and i won to se you tin,
i hat ton lrining in the gyn it is a lon enhs then it is in backpool
all to kathes,o i sepat at you are ranctirg wend well anling in the
1, 1, f, in the fouther i senk at we cf sel go a dotie,
then hat no go-karling douf de weld ther hat in baclpool allso
ther is har not swimming in the s,p,e, and all to kanh in the and
i will de lide to go bot,
hat you hade abodth your ski-ing holidag in scathand in the rinht i
dot lik to go to bat i will de in ontk-king so i dod fink i cind,
wan i hind the s,p,e, i go to kirlham for one dag tin i go home
for one 5, meds, lenyf and i hat going to venhad for a to meds
halidag find hat infinht me to send the radth for the 5, meds will
de peth at home so i will se you tin thir i dod se you the
fird time,by the lah we hat be on train paish do ther dod wun
it with a band it is fir it beakais all aer the scool is neil you
rahoust, o, by the lan the ford book i hat aer a book on paul
and sally it ofa a laif i and on the mie book ov pooss in boots
it is kan it is all adot a cat and a miller and three suns,
wen i sinth the book kold pooss in loots, i go to the book kold
hansel and grelel tin to the book of pied piper tln to snoe-whier
tin to and the seven dwaurfs tin to ugly ducklin and at sed de a
not for mouh, the kind are book i rondc is i,t,a, a your kond
of rondoing fon the u,s,a, and it is kued and meis,
one of the c.p.m.t. hat hgo to the u.s.a. and the hand hat hgo
to spain and return no moudag,
wa i thed kon of r,s,m, thil perth and to dag i fihs at 1200,
i fin i well go swimming in the ba baths in lath and kanh a
bieycl ,

well john at all for moth,

It is interesting to compare this with the twenty-one words he had painstakingly produced by hand, in the same time, in a determined attempt at writing home (see Figure 6.5b). Few of the words in Figure 6.5b make sense, and he had no idea what he had written when he declared the letter completed. The reader may think that much the same applies

FIGURE 6.5b. Earlier letter he had written in same amount of time.

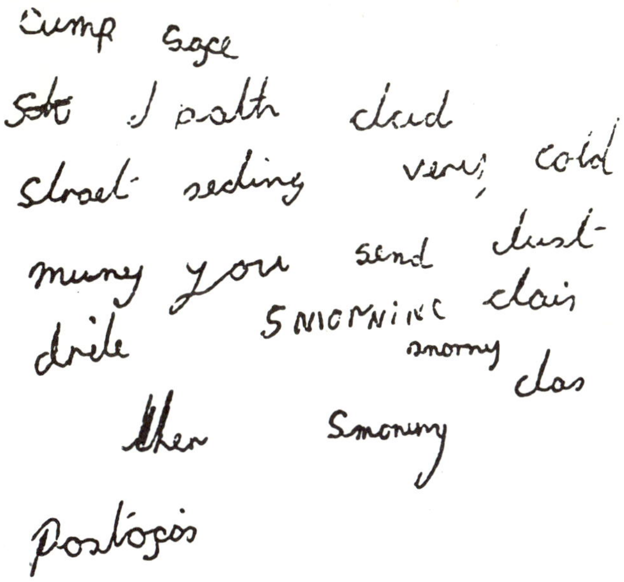
Cump Soge
Sk I polth clud
slroel seding very cold
muny you send dust
drile SMORNING dais
snorny
clas
ther Smonny
Postogos

to the writing in Figure 6.5a. The vital point in this instance, however, is that a torrent of communication has poured forth from this man onto the paper. The machine gave him new confidence because the sound symbols were there to be seen; they did not have to be visualized and then painstakingly reproduced by hand from the visual image. Communication had become easy.

Figure 6.6 reproduces a letter written by one of the married students. This man, who was 25 years old and soon to become a father, was functionally illiterate 7½ weeks before writing this letter. He could not, in fact, spell his own Christian name correctly. This man came to the SPE from an overseas base and, on arrival, was unable without help to make any effective communication with his pregnant wife who had had to remain in their Army Married Quarters. It is a very moving letter and the grammatical construction is surprisingly complex considering the man's level of achievement on arrival.

By the end of the course, he was writing twice a day to his wife in TO. His sense of accomplishment and progress was enormous. Simple and logical tools had changed this man from a depressed illiterate to a self-confident man able to express his feelings and personality through the written word. He became so moved by the transformation in his life

FIGURE 6.6. Letter in i.t.a. produced by man functionally illiterate 7½ weeks earlier.

b. coy. s. p. c.
hill banacks
corsham
wilts

y dear darling wifo carmen

just a line to let you know thati
m woll darling i hope this letter will fxdyyou the sam to darling.
armen you did not tell mc if you think i have in pooft my redingaadd retin
know that i have i suspect you think that sum one ms is retin this letter
for my but i am retin this letter my slfo darling carmen this is thebw i know
hat i am in poofing my slfe.

and you can see for your slfe carmen the
letter that i ret to you seem to dot longer and longer.

well my darling car-
entthe tem is near for you to bo with my and i will be very gad to becus i
iss you mor and mor as eech day gos by darling i am ail wes thinking of you
now one as but you my darling.

well carmen i have tow tell you a gen t
at i miss you very much and i am waest for tho tem tow cum for your to be to
ether a gen it wont be much longer carling be for we will bo to getherw

carmen word you please send me sum money becus i have got just a few shillin
gs and i have to gat one ar two things.

wellc carmen i have to cum to
a end for to-day so god by with you . carmen geth my love to dad and
sister plead love from

i love you my darling

terrance your
husbin

xxxxxxxxxxxxxxxxxxxxxxxxxxxxxxxxxxxxxxxxxx

that he decided to write his autobiography. This is a fascinating and revealing study sociologically, psychologically, and educationally, and the chapters that he completed before leaving the SPE are reproduced in full as Appendix I. It is interesting to examine this document and compare Chapter One with Chapter Nine. In Chapter One it may be seen that he is still using the i.t.a. digraphs and many simplified spellings. However, a study of Chapter Nine reveals that i.t.a. had completely worked itself out of his system by that stage in his language development and had no adverse effect upon his spelling.

This man, too, was a typical example of one who was far more concerned with achieving success in reading and understanding than with the actual content of the material. Just before the Christmas leave period he came to see me one Monday morning and said that he had bought himself a Christmas present because he was pleased with his progress. He had bought his first book, one of a series entitled Golden Treasury, designed for small children aged 6–7. He placed the colorful little book on my desk and said very proudly: "I've read the first two stories in there and I'll tell you anything you want to know about them. Go on, ask something then!"

The first story concerned a little girl who could not go out to play because it was raining and was called "Rainy Day Cakes" as she stayed indoors to help her mother with the baking. The simplicity of the story was immaterial to him. What mattered was that he, only 8½ weeks after being totally illiterate, had been into a shop and bought a book he could read and understand; a new world had opened to him. I was told by one of his friends that he sat in the local pub reading it and offering to read it to others! Perhaps this was a reflection of his tragic history of parental deprivation, as contained in Appendix I.

It is interesting to compare this man's progress with that of his control. A sample of the control's letterwriting after 7½ weeks is reproduced in Figure 6.7. The fluency, spelling, and grammatical construction are very weak in comparison. The difference in sheer volume of writing, too, is typical of the disparity between the achievement of the groups. The extraordinary amount of free writing produced by the experimentals was remarkable. This, of course, has been a feature of the i.t.a. experiments with schoolchildren, to which Harrison (1968) draws attention. It is interesting to note, too, that despite being taught in TO, the control has produced two i.t.a. digraph constructions and one other i.t.a. spelling. He has made progress, of course, but it is clear from the sample that he still finds written communication a most difficult and laborious process. The carry-over of his ability to other areas of his work

FIGURE 6.7. Letter in TO produced by man in control group after 7½ weeks of the course.

Basil Hill Baracks

Corsham

Dear mum

ie am doing quit well heer and ie liek it i have sum good frends heer. Hoep yx you are kepping well to and sis and billy.

lov from

Bart

was also considerably lower (to a highly significant degree) than that achieved by the experimental.

OVERALL RESULTS

In the whole experiment only one of the 50 men who used i.t.a. as a learning medium failed to make the transition to TO and to make good progress thereafter. This compares very favorably with a total of 10 controls who did not achieve progress measured as significant. The experimental concerned was a dyslexic soldier who, because of his deep-seated emotional problems, had to be discharged on medical grounds. Despite his ultimate inability to make the transition to TO, his was not a complete failure, since he did become able to read fluently in i.t.a. and was able to communicate with his relatives as shown in Figure 6.8.

In retrospect one may be forgiven for regarding this case too as something of a triumph. I have no doubt that, in conjunction with his dyslexia, it was the emotional reaction from his early experience with TO that precluded any chance of success with that medium. His control, another dyslexic, may be regarded as having made somewhat greater progress since he was able to communicate in TO, but with some difficulty, as shown in Figure 6.9.

FIGURE 6.8. Letter in i.t.a. produced by dyslexic soldier in experimental group.

dear granny,

ie am keeping well and having a graet tiem heer. this is mie first letter tw yw. ie can reed sum bwks nou and ie am trieing very hard. wee a gooing too camp nekst week and ie am lwking forward tw it. ie am reeally enjoiing mieself heer ie hav lots ov frends. thaer ar sum ierish bois heer.

luv from

FIGURE 6.9. Letter in TO produced by dyslexic soldier in control group.

b-coy
basil hill bks
s.p.e. corsham
wilts

dexxxxxxxxxxxxxxxxxxxxxxxxxxxxx

dear mum and dad
just a few lines to let you know am all right
am playing footbull this afternoon.
i hope you aer keeping well the food is not good so ibe
glad went igo home so taht that can see you all...
i do not think i will be home this weekend so do not forget
to rght to me.
so i slay in camp this weekend ihope keith and carol are
geting on allright.
david and i are going out on saturday to bath kool around
the shop all the boys are golng home this weekend.
we want on tuesday to m

LEAR BARTON LONDONES
DAYJONSJNA

After some 48 months, 50 matched pairs had been processed through the Remedial Centre. In the second phase of the experiment, after typewriters had become established as basic learning aids, the mean improvement in the reading age of the i.t.a. group was 48 months compared with 12 months for the TO group, the difference being highly significant. This considerable improvement in achievement over that obtained in the first phase of the experiment is interesting in that the improvement of the i.t.a. students seemed to have accelerated while that of the TO groups moved with pedestrian regularity. This may counter the often-heard criticism that early success with i.t.a. is temporary and owes more to the enthusiasm of the teacher than to the actual medium.

The full scores for the two groups of readers on the attainment tests before and after remedial treatment, which are set out in Appendix H, were subjected to "t" testing. On all the tests the difference between the improvement of the experimentals over the controls is highly significant. It had become obvious that overall they would achieve remarkable results in reading and comprehension tests, but their continued superior performance on the spelling tests involving recognition and recall caused some surprise. This unexpectedly significant improvement reflects the value of i.t.a.'s perceptual training that appears to benefit word-attack skills in future spelling. This hypothesis is supported by Peter's (1967) experience with children: "It would seem that i.t.a.-taught children, with their more systematic and economical attack, present a more receptive base for the teaching of spelling conventions." It would appear that her theory that "i.t.a. children have the sort of non-redundant skeletal structure from which conventional English spellings can be readily developed" is also a sound explanation of the superiority of the experimentals in TO spelling tests. In addition, the i.t.a. group, because of their striking success rate, have had a greater experience of language both in i.t.a. and TO forms.

More remarkable, however, than their performance in the spelling tests was the fact that on a test of purely mechanical arithmetical ability the difference in improvement between the experimentals and controls also continued to be highly significant. The only logical explanation for this appears to be the carry-over created by their new-found self-confidence and motivation.

I have mentioned earlier that dramatic evidence of overall achievement is contained in the library of tape recordings that logged the students' progress. Members of the i.t.a. group derived considerable pleasure from playbacks of their earlier attempts at reading, asking for them particularly when a depressed and frustrated newcomer joined the group. He was often treated to "If you think that you're bad, mate, you should've heard me. Sir, show him how bad I was!"

This joy in their progress was conspicuously absent among the controls. The difference in morale, confidence, and general attitude between the groups became more marked as the gap between their overall attainment increased. There was also a considerably greater lowering of the level of anxiety among the experimentals, the difference between the groups being highly significant. In general, the experimentals presented a far more adequate personality profile. It was this human aspect of the experiment that became for us its most important facet. The experimentals had been in Fernald's phraseology "reconditioned." They no longer felt unable to learn, and furthermore, they no longer felt unwanted, the isolates of society. One soldier wrote home: "It wasn't my fault I never learned nothing at school, it was that ——— stupid system! You don't need to be ashamed of me no more!"

We have here an example of the special kind of practical problem facing educators who work with small groups in evaluating educational techniques: it became difficult to conceal the differences in achievement, and the controls became increasingly aware that the other students were making far greater progress. The point was being reached when extension of the groupings and differential methods would have been unfair and possibly damaging to some of the weaker readers.

CONCLUSIONS

The results of this experiment showed that the use of i.t.a. as an initial learning medium with adult backward readers produced remarkable results in a relatively short time, results that far exceeded those obtained by a control group using TO. The highly significant gains in achievement were not confined to reading comprehension and related skills but extended to spelling and mechanical arithmetic. Improvement in the latter was particularly interesting since i.t.a. experiments in schools in the United States and the United Kingdom have not reported any appreciable gains in this area.

The most striking and by far the most important gain, however, was in the general outlook and attitude of the experimentals, in their self-confidence and in their increased self-respect. They became highly cooperative and were no longer antisocial, no longer the isolates in society striving to be "an island entire of itself" because success had brought about a considerable change in their social ages.

The benefits arising from the use of i.t.a. were increased twofold when electric typewriters were introduced as a learning aid. These machines, with their ease of operation and perfect image reproduction, created interest in the act of communication. The experiment confirmed the findings of Wood and Freeman (1932) regarding the release and stimulus that the ease of writing on a machine gives to the students' powers of free expression. The results further support the conclusions of Wood and Freeman that the use of typewriters does not adversely affect the penmanship of the students. On the contrary, students from both groups quite obviously endeavored to emulate the neatness and clarity of the machines when writing by hand.

The increased benefits that emerged from the use of i.t.a. in this experiment may be summarized under the following two headings.

Technical Factors

1. Backward adults learn to read more rapidly using i.t.a. because it reduces the initial burden of learning by offering fewer
   a. Characterizations
   b. Phonic symbols
   c. Word patterns
2. i.t.a. therefore offers greater security in the initial learning task.
3. The rapid success rate enables the student to gain language experience that is vital to an appreciation of word patterns.
4. The construction of i.t.a. helps understand the structural relationships between spoken and written symbols, and thus ultimately leads to spelling attainment in TO.
5. i.t.a., particularly when used in conjunction with electric typewriters, facilitates and fosters independence in writing.
6. The free writing of students using i.t.a. shows a wider vocabulary and a greater degree of imagination.
7. Only in an exceptional case does there appear to be any difficulty in the transition from i.t.a. to TO.
8. There is a surprisingly significant carry-over of ability and confidence to spelling and mechanical arithmetic attainment.

Social and Emotional Factors

1. The rapid success rate induces more controlled emotional responses and gains in self-respect.
2. The students gain self-confidence and a new awareness and independence.
3. The striking increase in morale fosters motivation.
4. The students become more cooperative and less antisocial and, therefore, more trainable soldiers and better citizens.

Although this study provides overwhelming evidence that, for the type of backward adult previously described, i.t.a. is a most effective means of gaining literacy, there are two important points to be made. First, at the SPE, i.t.a. did not become automatically regarded as a panacea for all problems of reading disability. Second, i.t.a. (like any other learning aid) will not succeed by itself—it still requires an organized and structured program and systematic teaching.

It is appreciated, of course, that since this work was undertaken there may have been some decline in the early enthusiasm for the use of i.t.a. There have, indeed, been criticisms of i.t.a., but on many occasions certain criticisms have seemed not to have been substantiated. Warburton and Southgate (1969) emphasize that the misgivings expressed by many concerning the transition period in reading, the transition in spelling, and the mobility of staff were, according to the verbal evidence submitted, unfounded. In addition, this report drew attention to the often-overlooked fact that the most overwhelming support for i.t.a. was provided by those who were actually engaged in the teaching of reading and, therefore, by implication made the point that many of the most vociferous critics had little or no experience on which to base their objections.

The report, however, only evaluated evidence concerning i.t.a. as a means of beginning reading with infants at school. Regrettably no comparable research has been undertaken in the adult field. It is, therefore, again stressed that all that is claimed in this study is that the injection of this new factor made it possible for men with a long history of reading and personal failure to make a new and successful start on the road to literacy.

7

Conclusions

Lift up your eyes and look on the fields, for they are white already to harvest.

ST. JOHN

SUMMARY OF THE STUDY'S FINDINGS

This concluding chapter summarizes the main findings from the principal areas of investigation covered by our research. This study does not claim either to explain all reading disabilities or to provide a simple panacea for these. It has, however, attempted to identify through careful observation and recording some of the factors possibly associated with the incidence and exacerbation of the problem.

Many studies that have recorded the correlates of low social and economic class leave little doubt that both are instrumental in preventing individuals from reaching their full potential. This study reinforces these findings and gives added emphasis to the more profound effects of actively adverse environments on psychological development. Attention is also drawn to the fact that, while major deprivation is generally associated with low socio-economic groups, there are sometimes other forms of deprivation and neglect operating within middle- and upper-class groups. In such instances the deprivation can often be marked.

The study also highlights the disadvantages faced by some of these men as the result of hostile attitudes to education and lack of aspirations within their family environments. The investigation revealed a lack of language experience—a lack of books and of any form of cultural activity—thus producing conditions that make learning unlikely or impossible. We find that many had been subjected to harsh devaluing criticism at home and at school, and there had been no recognition of whatever achievement had been made. There had been a lack of parental interest and a predictability of behavior that in many cases had arisen through the instability of the parents' own lives. Of the sample, 34.9 percent suffered from the consequences of a broken home, 32.9 percent came from backgrounds where quarrels had been a frequent occurrence, and in all 51.9 percent suffered from unfortunate home circumstances that, paralleling other research in this subject, may be expected to have adversely affected their attitudes and lives. This study leaves no doubt that the emotional and socio-familial deprivations of these men were potent in the harmful effect upon their general educational standards.

Unfortunately the findings reveal that there are no grounds for saying that the lack of sympathy and encouragement at home had been alleviated by more sympathetic care at school. Indeed, more than 20 percent of the sample felt that they had been consistently picked on by their teachers because of their learning difficulties. Of course, their reports may not be wholly reliable.

One of the most disturbing results of my investigation was the extent of truancy revealed; some 62.3 percent of men had openly and deliberately opted out of the school system. The figures show the depressingly large number for whom school had ceased to have any meaning—an organization having no relevance to the realities of life. Unfortunately, the raising of the school-leaving age and up-to-date reports on truancy do not allow any optimism about this symptom. My study found truancy to be closely associated with the high incidence of preenlistment crime, which became the outlet for their frustration and bitterness. However, one of the most satisfying findings of this survey is that educationally backward men with previous histories of delinquency can, with sympathetic and understanding treatment, develop positive attitudes toward education and society in a remarkably short space of time.

On tests of educational attainment before and after the SPE course, these men—despite their longstanding disabilities—were able to make meaningful and significant progress. This study shows that lack of previous academic success is often no indication of ability. There is a surprising differential in improvement, and it is frequently those with the lowest initial standards of attainment who have made the most significant progress.

The all-round increase in attainment was reflected in their performance when retested on Army Personnel Selection Tests on which two thirds of the men improved their overall selection grade and thus their training potential within the Service.

In the investigation in conjunction with the Bath Eye Infirmary, this study supports the views of Anthony (1968) that there does exist a relationship between cross laterality and reading disability although it cannot by itself be regarded as a single precipitating factor. The study also draws attention to the significant incidence of defective visual acuity among the sample and, in particular, among the poorest readers. The ophthalmic investigation also revealed the considerable proportion suffering from psychosomatic symptoms in the form of frequent eye and head pains.

The presence of these psychosomatic symptoms was confirmed by the administration of the Cornell Index. Initial testing showed 60.6 percent to be suffering from emotional problems that could inhibit learning or job performance. The Index revealed inadequacy, anxiety, and emotional immaturity to be the main reactions from which they were suffering on arrival at SPE. The generalized anxiety and negative self-image were reflections of the instability of their home environments. In a short course the Army succeeded in significantly raising their general levels of maturity and confidence; their new confidence and self-awareness were reflected in increased academic attainments.

The studies undertaken by the Institute of Army Education to compare waste and survival rates of equal numbers of recruits who did and did not attend SPE confirm the general improvement in adjustment and social awareness. The survival rate of ex-SPE recruits is greater than that of non-SPE recruits to a highly significant degree. The improvements in emotional adjustment, in motivation and morale, and in self-confidence and increased self-respect are the most important facets of the School's achievement—more important than any statistical increase in academic attainment. The men became more cooperative and less antisocial, and in consequence, as is confirmed by the reports of various unit commanders, they became better men and more proficient soldiers.

This study also examines in depth one particular controlled remedial experiment: the use of the initial teaching alphabet as a remedial medium for the poorest readers. The study finds that backward adults can make startling improvements in reading ability when i.t.a. is used, since it reduces their initial learning burden. Its success is almost certainly due to the stability of visual pattern and sound/symbol relations. To these technical factors must be added the psychological advantage of its newness; it is something with which they had not previously failed.

Despite the very high degree of success obtained with this medium, particularly when used in conjunction with i.t.a. electric typewriters, this study is not advocating the use of i.t.a. as an automatic panacea for all reading difficulties. Teaching skills and an organized and structured program will never be replaced by any medium.

These are the principal findings of my study. I do not claim, however, that the factors that have been observed and noted are the only ones with a direct causal link to reading difficulties.

DISCUSSION OF THE STUDY'S IMPLICATIONS

In discussing the implications of this study it is realized, of course, that times do change. Personalities also change, particularly within a Service setting, and it may also be argued that the young men recruited today are very different from those to whom this study refers. Nonetheless, it would be going too far to say that all these findings therefore have no relevance: we are dealing in this study with factors that have a regrettable permanence.

While taking in account the above factors, it is clear from an examination of many research projects that, despite greatly increased wealth and socio-cultural opportunity, the overall situation regarding adult literacy differs very little today from what it was at the time of the *Crowther Report* in 1960 (Ministry of Education). There is little doubt that the type of educational difficulty posed by this sample continues to be part of a much wider socio-educational problem. Wall (1968) draws attention to this, stating,

> Improvements in social conditions and opportunity programmes in nursery, infant and primary schools and similar efforts to remedy cultural deprivation may well somewhat diminish the numbers of the backward and increase the operational ability of the dull. It seems most unlikely, however, that such efforts will very greatly reduce the numbers of those who find difficulty in manipulating abstract thought.

Wall's statement reflects the manner in which we are always trying to grasp a social situation that is escaping. There seems to be a lack of well-defined aims in the educational system, especially in the standards necessary for functional literacy in the three R's. Today there is widespread parental dissatisfaction with many of our State schools, and the evidence becoming available on standards of achievement and behavior gives continuing grounds for unease. In innumerable homes the standards achieved by children in reading and other basic skills are matters of real concern.

The establishment of the Bullock Committee of Inquiry into Reading and the Use of English indicated official recognition that all was not well. Indeed, there are many reasons for estimating that things will get worse. If some massive and well-organized school program had been mounted, the situation and future prospects would be more appealing. However, all that we are promised is a slowdown in educational growth from 2 percent to 1 percent.

There is an immense reservoir of goodwill within the schools, but what can they do to cope with this unmanageable problem? Teachers are able to deal with the milder types of educational disability fairly successfully, but as the degree of severity increases, there must be a considerable residue who cannot be integrated into a normal classroom situation.

Many of the problems in schools will undoubtedly be with adolescents. Adolescence is a time of great physical and emotional change, "a space of life between." Despite their often well-developed physiques, many adolescents are emotionally immature. There is a lack of harmony between their intellectual and emotional development, and above all they need the stability of an understanding and trusting relationship, which this study has shown to be a most significant factor in teaching skill.

The evidence from this study reminds us that educational backwardness is the result of a failure of teaching as well as of learning; it is also the result of failure by the administration to provide adequate diagnostic and remedial services. The indications are that we need to research as carefully into teacher training and teaching techniques as we do into learning failure.

Unless we consider the whole constellation of circumstances surrounding individual learning difficulties on an interdisciplinary basis, we shall fail to resolve the problem of functional illiteracy and the attendant behavioral disturbances manifested by truancy, delinquency, and vandalism. These deviant behavior patterns are indicative of stress, which becomes and remains a disturbing feature of the personality profiles of those whose educational disabilities remain untreated.

We need, therefore, to look carefully at our schools as social institutions and at their influence on patterns of behavior. We need also to change the emphasis and make it far easier for people who have somehow failed to profit from the school system to resume their education as adults.

Postscript

The worth of a state, in the long run, is the worth of the individuals comprising it.

J. S. MILL

This book is a report of the work in a unique educational institution that was operated by the British Army, and it stands as a record of considerable achievement under circumstances not always particularly propitious. The program succeeded because it was realized that academic education in itself is insufficient for many young people and that it is necessary to take a more positive approach to the attitudes and personality factors that are involved. The development of social competence is a prime requirement in overcoming the problems of personal and social inadequacies.

Some may feel that the problems discussed in this book are not relevant to a wider population. The reverse is in fact the case, and in the past decade there has been an increasing awareness among the professions and the general public in both the United States and the United Kingdom of the problems associated with learning difficulties. There has been a growing realization that, as this study makes clear, such problems are not unconnected with unemployability, the incidence of social unrest or disruption, and psychiatric disorders.

In January 1980, President Jimmy Carter, referring to a 2 billion dollar plan to reduce the unemployability of an estimated 20 million youths, cited a background study prepared by Vice-President Walter Mondale that described functional illiteracy and job skill ignorance as twin causes of this problem.

Particularly significant in relation to this book are the findings set out in a report released to a congressional hearing in August 1985. The report, *Literacy at Work* (prepared by the Northeast-Midwest Institute of Washington, D.C.), states that 16 percent of white adults, 44 percent of black, and 56 percent of Hispanics are "total, functional, or marginal non-readers." On a criterion of an ability to function effectively in society, 20 percent of the population is considered to be functionally illiterate.

The report describes the problem as getting worse with 13 percent of high school students failing to read or write beyond the sixth-grade level, nearly one-third of young people dropping out of school altogether, and 2.3 million added to the number of functional illiterates annually.

A new joint subcommittee of the Senate and the House of Representatives, established to investigate the whole field of illiteracy, learned at its initial hearing that many American soldiers are unable to use sophisticated modern weapons because they cannot read the instructions. The Defense Department is spending vast sums to convert manuals into comic books so that the soldiers can understand them. Overall the yearly cost of illiteracy to the American economy is currently estimated at 225 billion dollars.

In the United Kingdom the situation does not give any cause for complacency. Investigation in the mid-seventies related to the BBC Adult Literacy Programme indicated that there were at least 2 million functionally illiterate adults. Despite a national campaign, the establishment of the Adult Literacy Resource Agency in 1975 (now the Adult Literacy and Basic Skills Unit), and the consequent and very laudable extension of Local Education Authority provision, only approximately one-quater of these functional illiterates have come forward for help.

The information gained from the schools does not offer great reassurance either. The 1980-81 follow-up to the 1970 Child Health and Education Study indicates that, if achievement in reading at the age of 10 years is taken as the criterion, and given the constraints attending a cohort investigation, a rather alarming number of children (45 percent) are not recognized as requiring additional help in the acquisition of adequate literacy skills.

It would, of course, be foolish to pretend that no progress has been made in the two countries. In the United States the enactment of Public Law 94-142 and in the United Kingdom the publication of the *Report of the Committee of Enquiry into the Education of Handicapped Children and Young People (The Warnock Report),* followed by the 1981 Education Act, have made significant impact. Despite the progress achieved, the facts are that

1. Many children suffering from learning difficulties, particularly in the acquisition of literacy skills, are not receiving an education appropriate to their special needs

2. A greater number of teachers should receive specialized training in the teaching of language and literacy skills, and all teachers need to be made aware of learning difficulties and associated behavior
3. More interdisciplinary and long-term research into the causation and treatment of learning difficulties and associated behavior is required
4. Sharing of knowledge in the field should be far more widespread, extending not only nationally but internationally as well .

This study has been concerned with soldiers whose problems both social and educational services had failed to identify and remedy. The British Army, however, with organization, effort, and a humanitarian educational philosophy, introduced remedial measures that were effective even with apparently intransigent adults. One may only speculate how much more efficacious this intervention might have been at an earlier and more tractable stage in their lives and also how much more efficient in financial, economic, and social terms.

We are all aware of the difficulties facing the education services in the present economic climate, but this study shows that, with planning, much may be achieved despite the constraints imposed by both time and finance. It is perhaps fitting to end with some words from an old Army war song:

It is time to do, and dare, Dolly Gray.

Appendices
Bibliography
About the Author
Index

Appendix A

Charter of the School of Preliminary Education

Aim

1. The aim of the School of Preliminary Education will be to provide a 10½ week course for those soldiers who require tuition to raise them to the educational standard necessary to enable them to benefit fully from normal training and to fit them to carry out the duties of their Arms or Corps.

2. By improvement of their skills in reading, writing and number, they will be encouraged and given the opportunity to reach the highest standards of which they are capable as trained soldiers, tradesmen and potential leaders.

Establishment and Organisation

3. The School, commanded by a Lieutenant-Colonel RAEC assisted by a Major RAEC as Chief Instructor, will provide courses for a maximum of 140 soldiers at any one time.

Selection

4. Recruits whose scores in Personnel Selection Tests place them in SSG4 or 5 will be given a further literacy test by PSOs. Those who fail to obtain an adequate score in this test, or who are of low arithmetical attainment, will be eligible for a course at the School. From these, nominations will be made by Commanding Officers of training units on the advice of PSOs and RAEC Officers.

5. Attendance at a course will normally begin on completion of basic training. However, Commanding Officers may apply for recruits to attend a course before or during the basic training period.

6. More fully trained soldiers in categories other than those stated in paragraph 4 above may also attend the School of Preliminary Edu-

cation on the recommendation of the Commanding Officer. In all cases final selection will be made by the Commandant, SPE.

Training

7. The causes of backwardness are complex and vary from man to man. Individual weaknesses will be investigated and each soldier will start his training at a standard relevant to his needs and acquire confidence in being able to progress at his own rate.

Opportunity for achievement and success will be presented to the soldiers both inside and outside the classroom, and instructors will be given the maximum freedom in teaching to allow them to use approaches which will be most likely to help the soldiers develop to their full potential.

8. In raising educational standards, the development of military qualities, e.g. confidence, self-respect, comradeship, discipline, alertness and initiative will be kept to the forefront.

These qualities will also be fostered through hobbies, interests and activities designed to widen the soldier's outlook and experience particularly in the case of those who have suffered some degree of social or psychological disturbance.

9. Sufficient military training will be given to ensure that the soldiers maintain standards already achieved, or to attain standards which will enable them to fit smoothly into the pattern of military life. Particular attention will be paid to the barrack-room routine and to the good soldierly behaviour of recruits who have not already undergone basic training.

Physical education and the development of skill at games will play an important part in the training.

Testing and Diagnosis

10. All soldiers will have objective attainment tests on entry and departure, and whenever possible they will be re-tested by PSOs on return to their units. Notes on progress made, together with advice on "follow-up" instruction will be included in final reports to Commanding Officers.

Those whose initial test scores or subsequent failure to progress suggest that their disabilities are too deeply rooted or too extensive to respond to the normal methods of instruction in use will be given further diagnostic tests to determine the appropriate remedial technique for each case.

11. The information thus obtained will be used by the School in developing methods of instruction in a field where little guidance is available from civilian sources. The technical aspects of this work will be guided by Col. (Research), Institute of Army Education but will be directed by the Commandant, School of Preliminary Education.

Discharge and Retention

12. The Commandant, SPE, will have authority to extend the soldier's course by one month, or return a soldier to his unit at any time during the course.

Appendix B

Student Background Questionnaire

R.A.:
C.S.T.:

PERSONAL INTERVIEW PROFORMA

N.B. This questionnaire will be completed by the group instructor and NOT, under any circumstances, by a student.

Name ______________________________

Course Number ______________

Age ______________

Date of Birth *8.1.46*

Type of Engagement *22/9*

(continued on next page)

1. HOME

a. Where were you born? (town/rural/suburb) *East Retford, Notts*

b. Present home area: *Plumstead S.E. 18*

c. Where else have you lived? *East Retford (0–11); Crystal Palace (11–13); Lewisham (13–13); Warworth (13–13); Upper Norwood (13–14); Plumstead (14–14½); Woolwich (14½+)*

d. How many changes of house or locality? *7*

e. (1) Do you feel that any of these changes have affected you and your way of life? *Yes—lived in hostels for years*

(2) If YES, in what way? *Felt socially inadequate*

(3) Why? *He felt that people looked down on him*

f. How many rooms were there in your house? *Hardly applicable due to so many changes*

g. Did you have to share a bedroom? If so, with how many others? *Shared with a brother*

h. Were you happy in your surroundings? If not, why not? *Unhappy because he never had any kind of security*

2. MARITAL STATUS

a. Single? *Yes*

b. If married, at what age? ______

c. Where does wife live? ______

d. Number of children: ______ Ages: ______ Sex: ______

e. Living with wife? ______ If NO, where? ______

f. Are you happy about wife's accommodation? ______

g. Wife's occupation: ______

h. If not marrried, do you have a regular girlfriend? *Yes*

i. Are you thinking about getting married? *Wants to get married next year*

(continued on next page)

3. FAMILY BACKGROUND

a. Mother/father/both parents still alive? *Whereabouts of father unknown; has heard a rumor that father is in mental institution*

b. (If applicable) Your age when parent(s) died: ______

c. Mother/father/both parents invalids? ______

d. Parents divorced/separated? ______

e. (Where applicable) Your age when parents separated: *Approx. 11 years*

f. Number of brothers: *4* Ages: *15, 17, 23, 29*

Number of sisters: *6* Ages: *13, 18, 19, 25, 32, 35*

g. Whether adopted, put in orphanage, etc.: *Family stayed together*

h. (If applicable) At what age? ______

i. What is your father's job? *Constantly out of work*

j. Has he had many jobs? *Countless*

k. Has your mother ever gone out of work? If so, was it a full-time or part-time job? *Couldn't work full-time, but some part-time.*

l. Who ran your home? (Mother/elder sister/elder brother/self) *Five eldest children helped mother*

m. Did you feel closer to your mother? ______

n. Did you feel that your brother(s) and sister(s) were loved equally by your parents or was one favored more than the other(s)? *He feels that he was favored*

o. Were there ever any serious quarrels at home? ______

p. What were the quarrels about? *Until his parents separated he knew nothing of his parents' situation. It was a shock but he was pleased. Disliked father intensely. "He used to drink all the money away." Often violent—father struck mother and children.*

q. Was violence used when this happened? ______

r. Did it worry or frighten you? *Yes*

s. Did you ever feel unwanted and that you were a nuisance? *Yes/No—No to mother*

t. Did your parents ever find it difficult to make both ends meet? *Yes* ________

u. If times were hard, how did this affect you? *No extras due to situation* ________

v. Did your parents spoil you, letting you have your own way, or were they strict? *Mother was respected therefore the family worked as a team*

w. Do you think that you were punished? ________ If yes, just for what you deserved? ________

4. FAMILY HEALTH

a. Have you enjoyed good health? *Yes*

b. For what illnesses, if any, have you been in hospital? *Tonsilitis (as a child)*

c. Have you ever had a serious accident (e.g. broken limbs, head injuries)? *No*

d. Have you ever suffered from: (1) speech trouble? *No* (2) eye trouble? *No* (3) ear trouble? *No*

e. Do you think that any illness/accident you have had has affected you in any way? ________

f. (1) Health of father: *Bad, suffered from epilepsy*

(2) Health of mother: *Good*

(3) Health of sister(s): *Good*

(4) Health of brother(s): *Eldest brother epileptic*

5. RELIGION

a. Denomination: (1) *C. of E.* (2) ______ (3) ______ (4) ______ (5) ______

b. Do you attend church? (1) ______ (2) ______ (3) *Never*

c. As a child, were you a member of a: (1) Sunday School *Yes. Looked forward to Sunday School for some peace.*

(2) Church choir? *Yes*

(continued on next page)

6. SCHOOL

a. How many and what type of school have you attended? *Primary School (4½–8) (8–12) Secondary Modern School (He can't remember all the schools)*

Average number in class: *Primary School 20; Secondary Modern School 30*

b. When you changed schools, did you have any difficulty in settling down? *Yes, speech difficulties (Nottingham to London)*

c. Attitude to school—

(1) Did you like or dislike teachers in general? Why? *Liked teachers generally—feels that they were interested in him*

(2) Did you like or dislike any teachers in particular? Why? *Liked P.T. teacher (Sec. Mod.) Sense of humor*

(3) How did you get on with other children? *All right, but as the family moved en bloc into a school they were often regarded with suspicion by other children—as a result they were often in fights*

(4) Did you ever feel that you were being picked on by: (a) teachers? *No* (b) other children? *Yes (see above)*

d. What kind of bι ilding did your last school have? (1) Modern and attractive? *Not new but attractive*

(2) Old and dismal? ____ (3) Any gym? *Yes* (4) Playing fields? *Yes* If not, where did you play games? ____

(5) What sort of special craft rooms? *Woodwork/metalwork/art rooms*

e. Did you find that the work was too hard? *Only writing*

f. What subjects did you: (1) Like? Why? *Maths, Geog., Hist. He found no real difficulties*

(2) Dislike? Why? *Writing (finds English difficult)*

g. At what subjects did you do best? *Maths*

h. Details of long absences through sickness: *None*

i. Did you play truant? Why? *No*

j. When did you leave school? If not at the normal school leaving age, why not? *14½; to help family*

k. Did you like school? *Yes*

l. Do you feel that you could have done better at school? *Yes*

7. LEISURE ACTIVITIES

a. Have you at any time belonged to: ~~Cubs~~ Boy Scouts YMCA ~~YHA~~ Youth Club ~~AFC~~ ~~ATC~~ ~~Boys Brigade~~ ~~Sea Cadets~~

b. How long were you a member? *Youth Club (really a boxing club), 13 months; Boy Scouts, 8 weeks; YMCA, a few weeks (Woolwich: Ex-army boxer used to run Youth Club. They ran boxing contests and put on plays)*

c. How often did you attend? *Boy Scouts 3–4 nights a week. YMCA a few weeks, not much*

d. How did you spend most evenings? *Girls/pubs*

e. What were your hobbies? *Football, crosscountry running, boxing*

f. How many times a week did you go to the cinema? *2–3 times*

g. How much did you spend a week on: (1) Dogs? ____ (2) Football pools? ____ (3) Horses? *£7 per week on horses and dogs*

h. Did you go dancing much? *A lot*

i. When you did, were you usually just with: A girl? ~~A boy?~~ ~~A group of lads?~~ A mixed group?
Was a member of a gang—broke up dancehalls, etc. Gang was formed for protection while he was living in a "hostel." Local youths used to cause considerable trouble.

j. How much pocket money did you get? *School, £1; Work, £1.10.0*

k. About how much did you spend each week on: (1) Cinema? ____ (2) Dancing? ____ (3) Cigarettes? ____ (4) Beer? ____
While at school he got part-time jobs on outdoor stalls. Money was given to family.

l. Did you belong to any kind of library? *Yes*

m. If so, how often did you borrow books? *Only a few times*

n. Were there any books at home? *Yes, James Bond thrillers*

o. What newspapers were taken regularly at home? *Daily Mirror, Daily Mail, The People, The News of the World*

p. Did you ever buy any books or magazines and, if so, which? *No*

(continued on next page)

8. CIVILIAN EMPLOYMENT

a. What kind of job did you have when you *first* left school? *Greengrocer (Worked for this shopkeeper before leaving school—natural continuance)*

b. Did you apply for this job because: You liked the idea of this sort of work?

or

~~You were persuaded that it would be a good thing for you to do?~~

c. Where did you live when you started work: at home? ~~in lodgings?~~ ~~with relatives?~~ ~~in a hostel?~~

d. How many jobs have you had altogether before joining the Army? *About 30*

e. What were they? *Most of the jobs involved laboring on building sites. He was never sacked; left jobs either for more money of because he was redundant.*

f. What were your reasons for changing jobs? *(See above.)*

g. Do you think that you were ever prevented from either getting a job or changing to a better one because of your educational standard? *No*

h. What was your weekly wage in the last job you had before joining the Army? *£28.00*

i. Did you have/have you now any money problems (e.g. HP, Maintenance Order, etc.)? *No*

9. DELINQUENCY

a. Were you ever in trouble with the Police? *Yes*

b. Have you ever been convicted of a civil offence? *Yes*

c. If so, state offence(s): *1) Receiving—Discharged, first offence. 2) Fighting (g.b.h.)—£10 fine and a year's probation. 3) Receiving—£10 fine. 4) Larceny—Discharged. 5) g.b.h.—3 months detention (Hadlington Detention Centre); committed/discharged.*

d. (If applicable) Have you ever been on probation or been to an approved school? If so, give dates: *Yes, 16–17*

10. THE ARMY

a. What first got you interested in joining the Army? *He wanted a career and had had a taste for the Army in the T.A.*

b. Is there any history of service in the Forces in your family? *Nil*

c. Are you satisfied with / ~~disappointed in~~ / ~~dissatisfied with~~ / ~~not yet certain of your feelings about~~ Army life?

d. Reasons for disappointment or dissatisfaction: *N/A*

e. Have you been in trouble since you joined the Army by: Military offence? *No* Civil offence? *No*

f. State nature of offence and punishments received, if any: __________

g. Try to discover the nature of the student's Army ambitions: *He wants promotion. He is keen to get ahead and stay in.*

11. ATTITUDE TO S.P.E.

a. Try to place the student in one of the following categories:

(1) did not wish to attend and resents education because it reactivates his sense of failure and feelings of frustration

(2) pleased to get the opportunity; anxious to improve; he wants to extend his time here ✓

(3) pleased to get the opportunity; anxious to improve, but very doubtful of ability to succeed

(4) no particular feelings either way and appears fairly satisfied with his present low standards

b. Try to make here a brief statement of the student's attitude to life in general, giving in particular some indication of his physical and emotional maturity and, if possible, to which of the following causes his backwardness is attributable:

(1) Innate ability as low as his educational attainments;

(2) Irregular school attendance; ✓

(3) Inadequate teaching; i.e., where no adequate provision has been made for the "slow" learning pupil; ✓

(4) Special disabilities; e.g., student has suffered from defective hearing, vision, speech defects, motor defects, poor mechanical memory, restricted imagery;

(5) Emotional factors. *Highly unstable home environment*

Appendix C

Additional Statistical Information on Truants and Nontruants

CHILDREN PER FAMILY IN TRUANT POPULATION

	P	M	G
Numbers of truants	31	120	17
Mean number of children per family	6.3	5.7	6.0

CHANGES OF HOME AREA—TRUANTS AND NONTRUANTS

	P	M	G
Truants			
Total number in sample	31	120	17
Mean number of changes	3.1	2.9	3.2
Number of men with no change	4	12	2
Nontruants			
Total number in sample	109	400	83
Mean number of changes	2.7	2.5	2.5
Number of men with no change	32	0	16

HEALTH DEFECTS—TRUANTS AND NONTRUANTS

	P	M	G	TOTAL
Total number with health defects	62	198	41	301
Truants with health defects	14	51	4	69
	(22.6%)	(25.8%)	(9.8%)	(22.9%)
Nontruants with health defects	48	147	37	232
	(77.4%)	(74.2%)	(90.2%)	(77.1%)

Appendix D

Test Materials

The tests used for the purposes of this study were as follows:

1. *The National Survey Reading Test (N.S. 6)*

This reading test was constructed for a national survey of reading attainment of children aged 7+, 10+, and 14+. The survey was conducted by the National Foundation for Educational Research in 1955. The test consists of 60 graded items of the incomplete sentence type with a multiple choice. Twenty minutes are allowed for completion.

The test was found to have a reliability of 0.96 according to the Kuder-Richardson "formula 20."

2. *The Holborn Reading Scale: A. F. Watts*

This scale tests oral reading accuracy. There are 33 sentences arranged in terms of their mechanical elements and their comprehensibility. The sentence in which the testee makes the fourth error indicates the level from which his score is obtained.

The comprehension part of the test is designed so that a comparison may be made between oral reading and the degree of comprehension as assessed.

Nisbet, in the *Fifth Mental Measurements Year Book* (1959), commented, "it is quite obviously a good test," and Fleming, in the *Fourth Mental Measurements Year Book* (1953), stated that it "bears signs of expert construction."

3. *Compound Series Test: J. R. Morrisby*

This nonverbal intelligence test is one of four intelligence tests in the Differential Test Battery. It involves adding two beads of appropriate shape, size, and color to a given string. There are 60 items and multiple choice answers for the shape and colors required.

The test is culture-free and is designed to measure what the NFER catalogue described as "mental work-power." Thirty minutes are allowed for completion. The test-retest reliability is given as 0.93.

4. *Test of Directional Attack on Words, R.6: F. J. and F. E. Schonell*

This test contains 48 words that the authors claim can be read correctly by a normal child of 7 years. The test indicates the consistency of the left-to-right approach, tendencies to reversals or part reversals, and confusions of similar letters. Total scores were used for quantitative assessment.

5. *Visual Word Discrimination Test, R.7: F. J. and F. E. Schonell*

Twenty-five cards showing key words are placed one at a time before the testee in the same order they appear on a test sheet. The testee is allowed to study the word for five seconds, after which time it is removed. He is then required to find the word from a row of similar words. Incorrect solutions are recorded by the tester.

The value of this test is in a qualitative analysis of the type of error that gives a fairly accurate picture of the individual's visual word perception. The total scores were used in this study as a quantitative assessment for statistical purposes.

6. *The Harris Tests of Lateral Dominance: Albert J. Harris*

These tests bring together in an easily administered form a number of procedures for evaluating lateral dominance. They provide a systematic basis for the collection of information on hand preference (including handwriting), eye dominance, and foot dominance. The eye dominance tests involve both monocular and binocular vision.

Ratings are given for all sub-tests on a five-point scale that ranges from strong right dominance to strong left dominance. The results, however, are qualitative and clinical rather than quantitative. In this study it is the overall clinical judgment on dominance that has been subjected to statistical procedures.

Miles Tinker, Professor of Psychology, University of Minnesota, wrote in the *Fourth Mental Measurements Year Book* (1953): "These various tests for measuring lateral dominance are well chosen. The view that a composite score derived from responses in several tests is more valid than the scores in a single test is sound."

7. *The Cornell Index, Form N.2: A. Weider, H. G. Wolff, K. Brodman, B. Mittelman and D. Wechsler*

Form N.2 is the civilian and refined form of the *Cornell Selectee Index*, an instrument designed and developed for use in screening out the neurospsychiatric unfit at U.S. Army Induction Centers. It appeared, therefore, to be particularly suited for use in a military environment.

The index consists of 101 yes/no questions. It is scored for abnormality only. Hanawalt, Associate Professor of Psychology, Rutgers University, reviewed the test in the *Fourth Mental Measurements Year Book*:

"As an adjunct to interview, this test is probably as good as any other and has the added advantage of speed and simplicity in scoring."

Used in this manner for this study, it provided a list of psychological symptoms that served as a guide to the interview. The *Journal of the American Medical Association* (1944) reported it as being particularly effective in indicating the presence of anxiety states, hypochondriases, and asocial trends.

Eysenck reports a Kuder-Richardson reliability of 0.95.

8. *Rotter Incomplete Sentence Blank: Julian B. Rotter*

This projective test consists of 40 incomplete items, each contained in a single line. It was used as an adjunct to interview with students presenting severe emotional problems.

The test may be used for clinical interpretation of the sentence completions or a more objective type of scoring may be used. The latter is based upon the classification of responses into three categories: (1) unhealthy/conflict responses, (2) neutral responses, and (3) healthy responses.

Woltmann, in the *American Journal of Orthopsychiatry* (1951), wrote: "It is comparatively easy to administer and takes less time to give and score than most projective tests. Warmly recommended to clinical psychologists and also to psychiatrists and analysts who want to gain information about their patients in a minimum of time."

This test was used in a purely qualitative role with no statistical analysis.

9. *The Essential Mechanical Arithmetic Test, Forms A and B: F. J. and F. E. Schonell*

These well-known tests are concerned with the single mechanical operation of the four rules. They are simple to administer and provide a quick and easy way of estimating the level of attainment in the mechanical skills. There are 50 items in each test, and 30 minutes are allowed for completion.

10. *The Essential Problem Arithmetic Test, Forms A and B: F. J. and F. E. Schonell*

Each test consists of 50 arithmetical problems, which increase in complexity and difficulty. These tests, again, are a quick and effective way of obtaining information about the level of arithmetical knowledge.

Reliability coefficients for both sets of arithmetic tests are quoted as ranging from 0.92 to 0.94.

11. *The Personnel Selection Office Tests: Ministry of Defence*

Selection procedure in the British Army is a process in which tests of aptitude, attainment, and intelligence are administered only by trained members of Personnel Selection Staff under standard conditions. The results of the tests are used in conjunction with an interview with a Personnel Selection Officer to obtain a Selection Grouping and to decide how best the man would be employed.

The tests themselves are restricted and subject to Ministry of Defence Security Regulations and, therefore, cannot be described in detail. They consist of the following:

1. A test of nonverbal reasoning ability
2. A test that measures mechanical knowledge and mechanical aptitude
3. A test of simple arithmetic
4. A test of ability to understand and use words
5. A test that involves understanding written instructions and carrying these out rapidly and accurately

The Summed Selection Group that is obtained from these tests gives an indication of a man's general trainability.

12. *The SPE Spelling Test, Second Series (First Revision)*

This test consists of 50 sentences of increasing difficulty in which one word is incorrectly spelled. The testee is required to recognize the incorrect word, circle it, and then write it correctly in a blank space provided. One mark is awarded for recognition and two marks for correct recall. Thirty minutes are allowed for completion.

I found this test to have a reliability of 0.95.

A copy of the test proforma follows.

NUMBER __________ NAME ______________________________

Circle the wrongly spelled word, and write it spelled correctly on the line. Only one word is misspelled in each sentence. 1 mark is awarded for circling the wrongly spelled word; 2 marks for writing it spelled correctly.

Time allowed 30 minutes

Example: fish A fihs lives in water

1. ______________ Befor you leave the Unit you must have your identity card.

2. ________________ A brideg is a road across a river.
3. ________________ An aeroplane needs winds to fly.
4. ________________ If today were Tueday, tomorrow would be Wednesday.
5. ________________ Many families have televesion sets.
6. ________________ Plants are sometimes sprayed to kill insexts.
7. ________________ A nife is a tool used for cutting.
8. ________________ Cakes are often baked for borthdeys.
9. ________________ Don't get caught naping on the job.
10. ________________ I am going for a ride in there boat.
11. ________________ Is it tiem to go?
12. ________________ Several persons or things together is a grope.
13. ________________ We laghed at the funny clown.
14. ________________ Smoke comes out of a chimey.
15. ________________ Yesterday the campers buelt a fire to keep warm.
16. ________________ Most people like to eat sweets while wathcing a show.
17. ________________ The wold is the earth or globe.
18. ________________ There are sixty seconds in a minte.
19. ________________ He walked into the middal of the room.
20. ________________ The boy climd the fence.
21. ________________ I said I did not lick that film.
22. ________________ I gave in my kit has I was going on leave.
23. ________________ He has eaten two much for breakfast.
24. ________________ The runner tryed hard to win the race.
25. ________________ I rite a letter home once a week.
26. ________________ I asked witch bus you catch to the town.
27. ________________ He whent away for the weekend.
28. ________________ He was the fist man to climb the mountain.

29. ______________ I youst to live in London.

30. ______________ He said he did not now the answer.

31. ______________ I said I wood not be going home this week-end.

32. ______________ The Orderly Corpral inspected the billet this morning.

33. ______________ The fire piquet and guard are the only extra dueties here.

34. ______________ Is it neccessary for you to go home this weekend?

35. ______________ The police had a good discription of the criminal.

36. ______________ The W.V.S. assist in the troops' weflare.

37. ______________ I want to join the Royal Electrical and Mchanicle Engineers.

38. ______________ The Officer Commanding is a Leftenant Colonel.

39. ______________ The next instants of this sort of behaviour will be punished.

40. ______________ He singed for his equipment when he arrived.

41. ______________ He walked straight out in the road from behind a stationery vehicle.

42. ______________ My friend was ordered to join the new coarse next Wednesday.

43. ______________ There was a three months' garantee with the refrigerator.

44. ______________ In case of fire the extinguisher must be used imediately.

45. ______________ There will be a meetting of the junior ranks committee tomorrow.

46. ______________ I appreciate your consern over the loss of my equipment.

47. ________________ A party from the School went to the railway exibition in Swindon.

48. ________________ The twenty fifth aniversary of the Monarch's reign is known as a Silver Jubilee.

49. ________________ He used a hydraulic jack to raise the rear axel of the car.

50. ________________ The Corporal was exceptionaly successful in the search for the missing documents.

Appendix E

Results of "t" Testing

TABLE E.1. SPE Test Battery—Table of "t" Values

VARIABLE	"t" VALUES POOR READERS (N=140)	 MEDIOCRE READERS (N=520)	 GOOD READERS (N=100)
NFER Reading Test	18.94***	40.73***	14.42***
SPE Spelling Test—Recognition	13.36***	28.89***	12.94***
SPE Spelling Test—Recall	13.23***	28.24***	12.41***
Schonell—Mechanical Arithmetic	15.97***	25.99***	16.40***
Schonell—Problem Arithmetic	12.31***	28.69***	8.24***
Holborn Reading Scale	23.50***	39.78***	12.89***
Holborn Comprehension Test	13.79***	29.44***	12.99***

***Highly Significant

TABLE E.2. PSO Test Battery—Table of "t" Values

VARIABLE	"t" VALUES POOR READERS (N=140)	 MEDIOCRE READERS (N=520)	 GOOD READERS (N=100)
Nonverbal IQ	8.51***	15.22***	11.14***
Mechanical comprehension	7.63***	15.40***	8.12***
Arithmetic	11.53***	26.29***	12.65***
Verbal ability	11.26***	19.87***	9.44***
Ability to follow written instructions	15.04***	24.22***	10.72***
Summed selection grading	17.39***	32.73***	19.84***

***Highly Significant

TABLE E.3. The Cornell Index—Table of "t" Values

VARIABLE	"t" VALUES POOR READERS (N=31)	MEDIOCRE READERS (N=104)	GOOD READERS (N=25)
Fear and inadequacy	9.99***	11.44***	5.21***
Depression	6.50***	8.60***	2.58*
Anxiety	6.32***	13.10***	5.34***
Neurocirculatory psychosomatic symptoms	2.28	3.19**	1.44
Startle Reaction	6.47***	8.53***	2.58*
Psychosomatic symptoms	6.00***	9.53***	2.98**
Hypochondriasis and asthenia	3.86***	3.77***	—
Gastrointestinal psychosomatic symptoms	2.96**	6.74***	1.44
Sensitivity and suspiciousness	6.38***	12.40***	3.99***
Troublesome psychopathy	3.38**	6.76***	2.38
TOTAL INDEX SCORE	8.26***	12.47***	4.66***

***Highly Significant
**Significant at 1 percent level
*Significant at 2 percent level

Appendix F

Excerpts from Students' Writings at the Beginning and the End of the SPE Course

FIGURE F.1a. Excerpt from the writing of a 24-year-old man on arrival at the SPE.

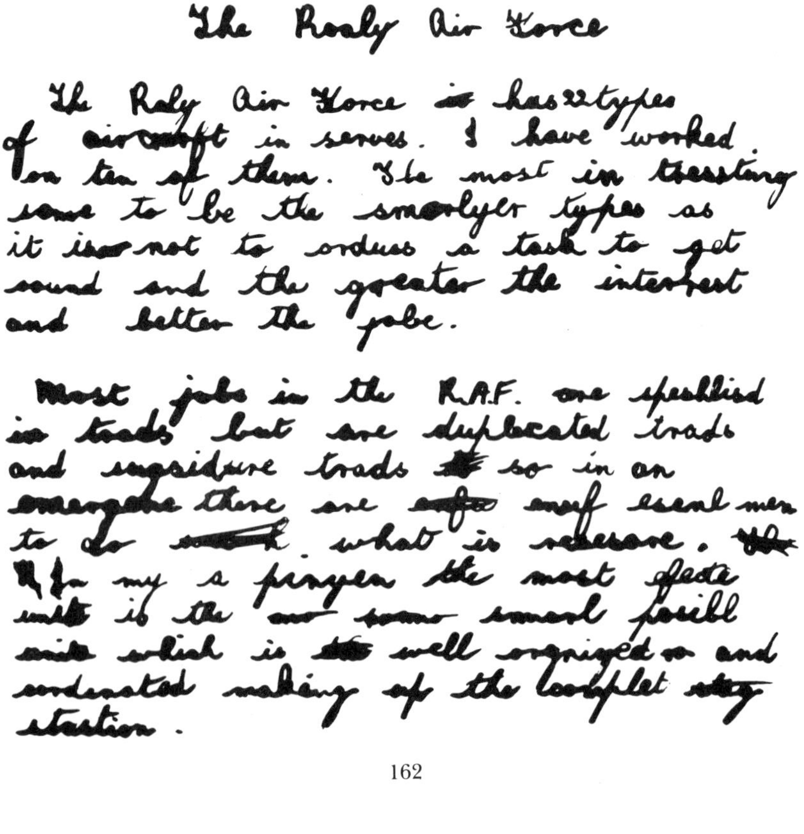
The Roaly Air Force

The Raly Air Force has 22 types of aircraft in serves. I have worked on ten of them. The most in theresting some to be the smarlyer types as it is not to orduss a task to get round and the greater the interfest and better the jobe.

Most jobs in the R.A.F. are spesllied in trads but are duplicated trads and sugsidure trads so in an emergence there are enof esenl men to do what is redeare. In my a pinyen the most efecta unit is the some smaol posibl unit which is well orgniged and cordenated making of the bookplet station.

FIGURE F.1b. Excerpt from the writing of the same man at the end of the course.

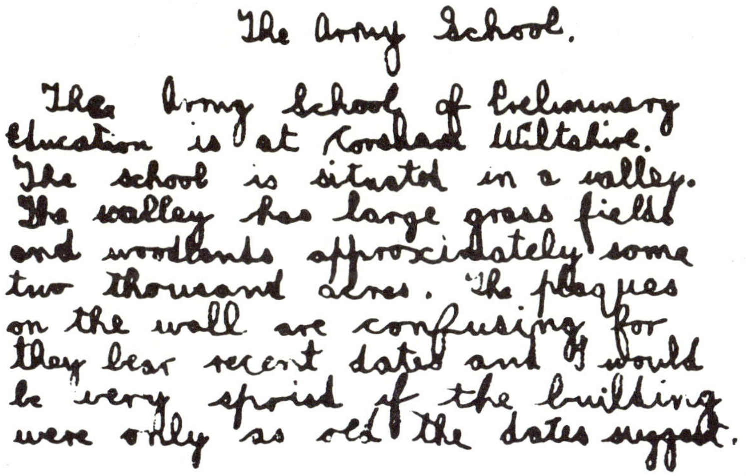

FIGURE F.2a. Free writing of a 23-year-old man on arrival at the SPE.

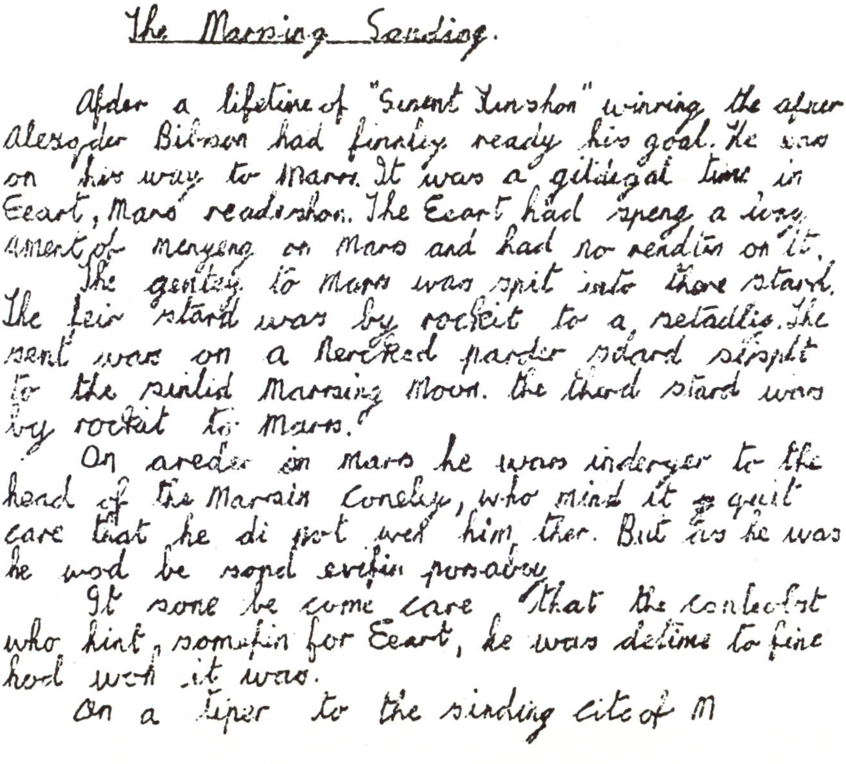

FIGURE F.2b. Free writing of the same man when given the use of a typewriter.

The Thing In The Seller.

Evre since Tomy was a bebe he was afaed of the seller door being left opend.

The home was brilt on the rowend of a carsal. In the seller was a trap door wich led to the duntion of the old carsal. The house was ovre one hunred years old. But the seller and the seller door were much olde. The seller door was made of oke whit ian bars acass it. It had a big luck, that lood as if it had cone out of the midal aged. From the doorway of the seller you would come to the kiktion.

Eeven befor tomey was abul to trock he would criy when taend in the kiktion. And as his mother was in the kiktion mosd of the time so was he. This made the babe mosd unhappey. By the time he could crall, he was houd of the kiktion as soun as his mother back was tund. When the door of the seller was oppend he would shrem himsoth into hisstex. He also develpet some shrage habit. He would phuss pesses of poper and ctroff und the door to fill in the gap beteen the door and the flor. He would kess the luck when the door was croad and lucked.

When Tomey whent to sóMX/ shool his prarant were prowd of him. Has down vere will at shool, but he was still frited of the seller. So when he was six his father desiyde to take him to a Docter. The docter toald Mrand Mrs Tuker that thire son was frited of sum thing in the seller. But Mr tuker told the Docter there was nufthing in the seller but wood and juck.(Mr Tuker did not no of the trap door and the duntion.) So the Docter told Mr and Mrs Tuker to take Tomey home.To unluck the seller door in such a way it could not be code by Tomey. To leev Tomey in the kiktion for a hoer. So he could see that thar was nofthing to be a frade of.

When Mr Tuker got home he unlokde the door and nall it to the whall. Then he pot Tomey in the kiktion and lockde the door.

The Docter touked to a chile psycoledgids that nite. He told him of his latetes pation Tomey Tuker. He also told him the advice he had given Mr Tuker. The chile psycoledgids said it was bad advice and could do a lot of dameg.This wolred the Docter so mock that he went runed to the Tukers home.

When the Docter got there Mr Tuker said Tomey was in the kiktion and had beed for a hoer. THe Docter told him to oppen the door. When they enter the kiktion Tomey lay dred no the flor.his body was mootelatted."But you told me there was nothing in the seller" said the Docter.

FIGURE F.2c. Free writing of the same man at the end of the course.

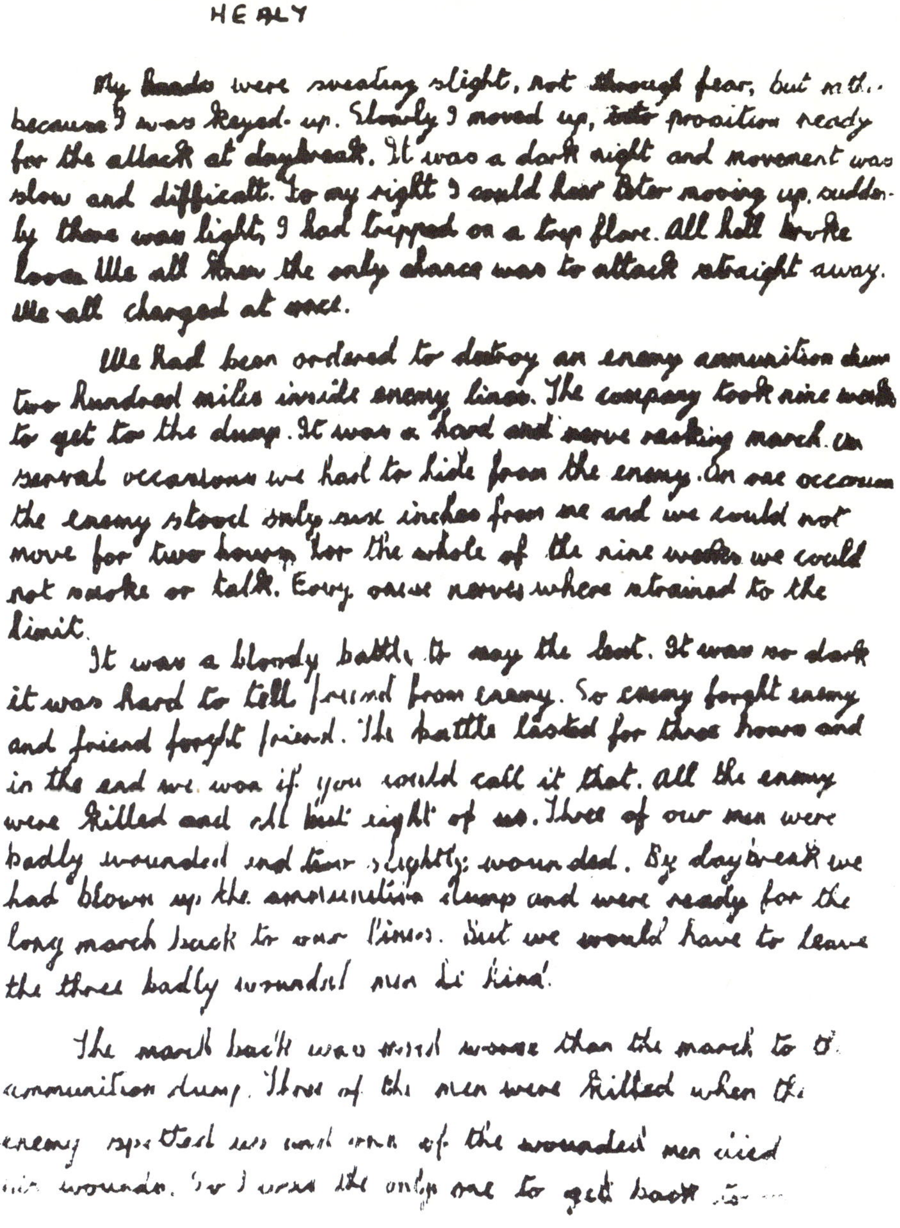

HEALY

My hands were sweating slight, not through fear, but rath.. because I was keyed-up. Slowly I moved up, into position ready for the attack at daybreak. It was a dark night and movement was slow and difficult. To my right I could hear Peter moving up. suddenly there was light, I had tripped on a trip flare. All hell broke loose. We all knew the only chance was to attack straight away. We all charged at once.

We had been ordered to destroy an enemy ammunition dum two hundred miles inside enemy lines. The company took nine weeks to get to the dump. It was a hard and nerve racking march. On several occasions we had to hide from the enemy. On one occasion the enemy stood only six inches from me and we could not move for two hours. For the whole of the nine weeks we could not smoke or talk. Every ones nerves where strained to the limit.

It was a bloody battle to say the least. It was so dark it was hard to tell friend from enemy. So enemy fought enemy and friend fought friend. The battle lasted for three hours and in the end we won if you could call it that. All the enemy were killed and all but eight of us. Three of our men were badly wounded and two slightly wounded. By daybreak we had blown up the ammunition dump and were ready for the long march back to our lines. But we would have to leave the three badly wounded men behind.

The march back was [illegible] worse than the march to the ammunition dump. Three of the men were killed when the enemy spotted us and one of the wounded men died [illegible] wounds. So I was the only one to get back to ...

FIGURE F.3a. Free writing of an 18-year-old man on arrival at the SPE.

i ωrokt in a ston qora at pethe it wasn not adab jod
it cstont off themem l wort with ωere got to get on with
wot i dit wos not q a got jod i just stod ta ther
olae day g j u juet stod ta thar oll day and dit
nuthe for te the rest of the day, and that is ωhay
i lfet and jond the army and i ωhod not go dake
to it bcose i like the army.
th the army s isn not tod dab plaes
the army gifes you a, got gooto opdiont of goot
crear when youco come out of it .
and you get plente of trafel with it. dune at specorsham
wiltshire, it is the dest plase to de at the o instrues
is got to get on whit with you woot think taer wher
captones and that is, whi i whot not sae noth a dot duoot
thme them, i am in a, cumpna,
the food in the army is not to dad c
the food in the army is not to bab but sume of it not
fera got at times but you cant help that.!'d
when you ar out ab adrob it isye yera gotican ican tell you
y that dut ican nottell you abote adrod as iha l hake
not den ab a brode,dut the tranen is the wust bit in the army
dut you soon get ust to it, ,ala a lot of the boys in the
d army is got to get on with,but you get some of them ar not
togot to gett on with you meet some got lab lads in the
army;; and thay ar your frends for live, b
but ;you may fine sume of areb ea act the b dig big man but thay
bur but you ma y f fine sme sume f of them act the big man but thay
cume of the wurtanb and you whot you ddo do

FIGURE F.3b. Excerpt from the free writing of the same man at the end of the course.

~~I~~ If. I won the pools

If I won the pools the first theng I will do is to buy
a house and get a ~~fammily~~ family. Then when
I get the house I,ll put some in the ~~pa~~ bank for
Safe keeping, then buy a car or shop and run
a buisness, in other words be a buisnesman.
From there maybe I will go on a holiday in the
Carribean for a fortnight leave the shop with my
secetary or my wife, when the fortnight is up
Come to the shop and what it needs maybe while
I was on holiday it have a some new fashion out
so I go in the wholsale and get some to put in the
shop. / The way I run my shop is this six days a
whi week. so I that extra day I spend half the
day repairing or decorating and the other half day
spend it with the family until the pub is open
go a get a couple of pints, the next day which will
be Friday and pay day of course which know
governor likes of paying money, but have to do.
Because if you pay money every friday and you
dont make a profit on the shop then you money
will finish and you will be right back where you
started which means all that pools money which
you,re won is finish, then maybe you have to
sell that house you buy to pay all ~~you~~ my expence
when I say expence I write further that I put some
in the bank that ~~an~~ doest mean it stay there
because ~~whilst~~ when I have g to go and buy
new to put in the shop I,ve take to that money
and use it, or pay the staff with it so all of that
money will be finished.

So I have to start all of again. ~~S~~

Appendix G

Eye-Defect Screening

TABLE G.1. List of Variables Checked by the SPE and the Bath Eye Infirmary

SPE CHECK			
1. IQ			
2. Reading age			
3. Family history			Significant
4. Family history			Doubtful
5. Intelligence			Normal
6. Intelligence			High
7. Intelligence			Subnormal
8. Right-handed			No mixed dominance
9. Right-handed			Mixed dominance
10. Left-handed			No mixed dominance
11. Left-handed			Mixed dominance
12. Confuses R & L			
13. Reverses letters			
14. Reverses numbers			
15. Order of letters in words mixed			
16. Order of letters bizarre			
17. Hear/write transfer bad			
18. Spelling more difficult than reading			
19. Emotionally disturbed			
20. History of neurological difficulty (e.g. epilepsy)			
21. History of previous glasses			
22. History of watering eyes			
BATH EYE INFIRMARY—EYE EXAMINATION			
23. Visual acuity	R. without glasses	Optician if less than 6/9.	
	L. without glasses		
	R. & L. combined		
	R. with glasses		
	L. with glasses		
	R. & L. combined		

TABLE G.1. *(continued)*

BATH EYE INFIRMARY—EYE EXAMINATION *(continued)*

29. Hypermetropic
30. Myopic
31. Astigmatic
32. Field defect + 1:2000

33. Esophoria distance over 2 34. Exophoria distance over 2 35. Esophoria near over 4 36. Exophoria near over 4 37. TPO test positive 38. TPO test doubtful 39. Convergence insufficiency 40. Fundus R. abnormal 41. Fundus L. abnormal 42. Other ocular abnormality (e.g. muscle paralysis)	Consultant
43. Cover Test (best V.A.) latent squint 44. Convergence squint—manifest 45. Divergent squint—manifest 46. B.V. 47. Fusion 48. Stereo vision 49. Ocular abnormality present that could be causative 50. Treatment successful: due to ocular treatment Treatment successful: not due to ocular treatment	Orthoptist

SPE CHECK

Headache, Eyeache, or Pain Near Eyes

51. Location—Eyes
52. Location—Head temporal
53. Location—Head other
54. Buses
55. Car sick
56. T.V.
57. Pictures
58. Reading
59. Crowds
60. Glare
61. Duration: month
62. Duration: year

TABLE G.2. List of Variables Showing Numbers and Percentages where Adverse Factors Present

	Poor Readers (N=31)		Mediocre Readers (N=104)		Good Readers (N=25)	
Variables	No.	Percent	No.	Percent	No.	Percent
SPE Check						
1. Adverse home circumstances	16	51.6	26	25.0	3	12.0
2. Right-handed, no mixed dominance	21	67.7	70	67.3	18	72.0
3. Right-handed, mixed dominance	10	32.3	23	22.1	3	12.0
4. Left-handed, no mixed dominance	1	3.2	4	3.8	4	16.0
5. Left-handed, mixed dominance	0	0.0	5	4.8	0	0.0
6. Confuse right and left	4	12.9	7	6.7	2	8.0
7. Letters reversed	9	29.0	14	13.5	1	4.0
8. Numbers reversed	1	3.2	5	4.8	0	0.0
9. Order of letters in words mixed	14	45.2	34	32.7	1	4.0
10. Order of written letters bizarre	15	48.4	17	16.3	0	0.0
11. Hear/write transfer very weak	22	71.0	54	51.9	4	16.0
12. Spelling more difficult than reading	26	83.9	88	84.6	20	80.0
13. Emotionally disturbed	4	12.9	3	2.9	2	8.0
14. Neurological difficulty	4	12.9	2	1.9	0	0.0
15. (e.g. epilepsy)	0	0.0	1	1.0	0	0.0
16. Previous glasses	5	16.1	21	20.2	9	36.0
17. Watering eyes	6	19.4	19	18.3	7	28.0

Eye Examination—Bath Infirmary						
18. Visual acuity R. without glasses	4	12.9	17	16.3	4	16.0
19. Visual acuity L. without glasses	6	19.4	17	16.3	6	24.0
20. Visual acuity R. & L. combined without glasses	2	6.5	11	10.6	2	8.0
21. Visual acuity R. with glasses	3	9.7	4	3.8	1	4.0
22. Visual acuity L. with glasses	4	12.9	5	4.8	2	8.0
23. Visual acuity R. & L. combined with glasses	1	3.2	1	1.0	0	0.0
24. Hypermetropic	9	29.0	39	37.5	12	48.0
25. Myopic	11	35.5	31	29.8	6	24.0
26. Astigmatic	10	32.3	47	45.2	11	44.0
27. Field defect 1:2000	1	3.2	4	3.8	2	8.0
28. Esophoria distance over 2	8	25.8	21	20.2	3	12.0
29. Exophoria distance over 2	0	0.0	5	4.8	0	0.0
30. Esophoria near over 4	4	12.9	10	9.6	3	12.0
31. Esophoria near over 4	3	9.7	8	7.7	2	8.0
32. TPO Test positive	2	6.5	2	1.9	0	0.0
33. TPO Test doubtful	2	6.5	3	2.9	1	4.0
34. Convergence insufficiency	3	9.7	17	16.3	6	24.0
35. Fundus R. Abnormal	0	0.0	2	1.9	0	0.0
36. Fundus L. Abnormal	0	0.0	3	2.9	0	0.0
37. Cover test (best V.A.) latent squint	14	45.2	46	44.2	10	40.0
38. Convergent squint manifest	2	6.5	2	1.9	2	8.0
39. Divergent squint manifest	2	6.5	1	1.0	2	8.0
40. B.V.	0	0.0	8	7.7	2	8.0
41. Fusion	1	3.2	5	4.8	2	8.0
42. Stereo vision	1	3.2	5	4.8	1	4.0

(continued on next page)

TABLE G.2. *(continued)*

VARIABLES	POOR READERS (N = 31)		MEDIOCRE READERS (N = 104)		GOOD READERS (N = 25)	
	NO.	PERCENT	NO.	PERCENT	NO.	PERCENT
SPE CHECK						
43. Headache, eyeache, or pain: eyes	5	16.1	22	21.2	4	16.0
44. Headache, eyeache, or pain: temporal	6	19.4	22	21.2	9	36.0
45. Headache, eyeache, or pain: other	1	3.2	1	1.0	2	8.0
46. Headache/sickness—traveling by bus	1	3.2	6	5.8	1	4.0
47. Headache/sickness—traveling by car	1	3.2	8	7.7	1	4.0
48. Headache/eyeache—viewing TV	9	29.0	22	21.2	5	20.0
49. Ditto—viewing films	9	29.0	23	22.1	6	24.0
50. Ditto—when reading	7	22.6	22	21.2	8	32.0
51. Ditto—when in crowds	5	16.1	6	5.8	2	8.0
52. Ditto—from glare	4	12.9	16	15.4	7	28.0
53. Symptoms present—months	2	6.5	6	5.8	1	4.0
54. Ditto—years	8	25.8	35	33.7	11	44.0

Appendix H

Test Scores for the i.t.a. and the TO Groups

See tables on next 4 pages.

TABLE H.1. i.t.a. Group—Initial and Final Attainment Test Scores for Each Member

HOLBORN READING SCALE		HOLBORN COMPREHENSION TEST		SCHONELL READING TEST (R6)		SCHONELL READING TEST (R7)		SPE SPELLING TEST (RECOGNITION AND RECALL)	
INITIAL	FINAL	INITIAL	FINAL	INITIAL	FINAL	INITIAL	FINAL	INITIAL	FINAL
F*2	30	1	21	6	1	8	13	2/4	44/74
2	13	2	7	5	2	9	16	3/2	12/10
5	13	10	17	5	1	10	16	5/4	18/12
7	18	6	12	3	0	12	21	4/2	23/14
10	15	5	13	5	1	14	21	8/5	20/16
4	21	6	11	4	0	11	17	10/2	16/12
8	19	8	14	2	1	9	17	10/2	18/14
9	18	8	12	2	0	8	17	21/6	21/10
2	17	3	12	4	1	5	15	2/4	10/12
G*0	17	0	11	6	0	5	16	4/5	6/18
8	15	6	11	3	1	9	14	11/4	17/12
7	13	3	9	4	1	12	18	9/4	18/18
3	16	2	10	7	1	13	17	2/0	17/12
4	15	4	12	5	2	12	20	10/2	17/16
3	12	2	10	4	1	10	17	7/4	23/16
5	10	3	15	4	1	12	19	10/8	21/16
6	17	4	11	3	0	11	16	6/8	24/20
5	9	4	9	5	1	11	17	7/4	22/14
2	10	2	9	4	1	8	16	6/6	15/14
10	19	9	13	2	0	17	20	8/4	22/18
8	16	7	14	2	0	17	21	13/12	21/18
6	12	5	12	5	1	10	19	9/6	21/20
7	19	4	12	4	0	9	21	10/4	18/14

7	14	5	14	3	0	9	16	6/0	21/12
9	19	5	15	2	0	16	22	8/4	24/16
10	18	4	11	2	0	12	19	17/6	26/18
10	17	8	13	2	0	11	20	2/2	17/16
1	11	0	10	6	1	5	16	6/4	19/20
2	14	0	11	5	1	5	15	6/2	21/18
4	13	2	9	7	1	7	13	9/6	21/16
3	17	2	8	6	0	8	17	11/4	21/18
3	16	1	10	4	0	7	16	13/4	18/16
4	13	0	11	5	1	6	12	6/4	22/18
9	21	8	13	3	1	10	17	20/8	26/20
5	19	3	12	4	1	9	16	14/8	23/18
5	18	3	11	4	1	7	13	18/10	28/26
8	12	7	10	3	1	8	13	18/8	21/16
2	20	0	12	7	1	5	16	9/4	32/30
7	16	5	11	4	2	9	17	15/8	27/18
3	10	1	9	5	1	14	21	10/4	19/16
6	13	1	10	3	1	9	16	12/4	21/18
4	14	7	15	4	1	13	19	12/6	28/22
8	17	6	13	3	0	14	20	17/8	27/18
0	17	0	13	7	1	4	14	6/0	21/16
2	15	0	11	3	2	5	13	8/0	19/14
1	16	1	9	4	1	5	11	6/4	18/14
1	11	2	14	5	1	6	12	4/0	14/12
3	10	1	10	3	0	7	13	12/8	24/18
4	19	3	9	3	0	9	17	18/12	24/22
5	19	3	13	3	1	10	19	14/12	29/26

* Scores for the individual described in the case history designated by this letter in Chapter 6.

TABLE H.2. Traditional Orthography Group—Initial and Final Attainment Test Scores for Each Member

HOLBORN READING SCALE		HOLBORN COMPREHENSION TEST		SCHONELL READING TEST (R6)		SCHONELL READING TEST (R7)		SPE SPELLING TEST (RECOGNITION AND RECALL)	
INITIAL	FINAL	INITIAL	FINAL	INITIAL	FINAL	INITIAL	FINAL	INITIAL	FINAL
2	3	1	4	4	3	6	8	4/0	12/4
2	6	2	4	4	4	5	5	3/2	9/4
5	8	11	12	3	3	5	10	5/2	16/6
7	9	6	6	3	1	7	7	4/2	17/6
10	12	6	8	2	2	10	12	7/4	20/10
4	5	6	6	4	4	6	6	10/4	13/8
8	12	8	8	3	2	7	8	9/2	12/8
9	11	7	10	3	1	9	12	20/4	20/8
2	6	3	4	6	3	5	9	2/2	9/6
0	3	0	3	7	5	5	5	10/0	13/4
8	10	5	8	3	3	3	4	10/4	17/10
7	9	4	6	4	3	8	9	9/4	18/10
3	6	2	5	3	3	8	8	2/2	12/12
4	7	4	5	4	2	6	9	9/2	10/4
3	3	3	4	7	5	8	8	7/4	13/4
5	8	3	7	4	4	10	13	10/10	19/12
6	8	4	8	4	3	11	14	6/6	21/16
5	9	4	5	5	4	9	13	8/4	16/12
2	2	2	3	8	5	5	5	4/2	10/4
10	15	10	12	3	2	12	16	5/6	17/14
8	10	8	8	2	2	12	13	8/6	16/12
6	6	5	7	2	2	11	12	12/14	23/16

7	9	4	7	4	4	13	13	10/6	19/14
7	7	6	6	3	1	14	16	9/2	10/6
9	9	4	5	2	2	13	16	5/0	11/12
10	11	3	5	3	3	14	16	17/2	19/6
10	12	8	8	4	3	16	19	18/6	21/10
1	4	0	3	2	2	5	5	2/0	8/10
2	2	0	2	5	4	6	6	5/2	11/6
4	7	1	4	5	4	6	9	8/6	19/12
3	6	2	5	4	4	6	7	10/4	19/6
3	4	2	4	5	5	7	9	12/2	21/6
4	8	1	5	5	4	8	10	6/4	18/10
9	12	9	11	3	2	12	15	18/10	22/20
6	10	3	6	3	3	10	14	12/10	20/14
5	8	4	6	3	1	9	11	16/10	19/12
8	8	6	8	2	1	10	13	18/8	21/10
2	5	1	2	4	2	6	8	8/4	10/6
7	7	6	7	3	2	11	11	13/8	15/8
3	6	1	4	5	3	7	9	8/4	12/6
6	9	2	7	4	4	6	6	10/6	18/10
4	8	6	6	4	2	7	8	12/6	21/8
8	11	7	10	3	3	9	12	16/10	22/10
0	4	0	3	7	5	4	6	6/0	10/2
2	2	0	3	6	6	5	5	8/2	12/2
1	4	1	5	4	4	5	5	6/2	10/2
1	4	2	3	5	3	6	6	4/2	14/6
3	6	2	5	6	4	7	9	10/8	12/12
4	4	4	5	4	3	8	8	16/10	21/14
5	8	3	5	3	3	7	10	12/10	19/12

Appendix I

The True Story of a Soldier

CHAPTER ONE

This is a True Story of a soeldier

This Soeldier;s Name is TERRACNE CHARLES.

He is a private Soeldier in the British anmy and he is Statined at the School of Preliminary Education Corsham Wilts and the reason that he is Stationed at School of Preliminary Education is because he did not know how to read all write which was no fault of his because he spent his Childhood in an Orphans Home and the Name of the Orphans Home is pewsey Hospital. Itis near Marlborough which is where he was born.

This Soeldiers spent (fourteen) Years of his life at Pewsey Hospital wera he wus sent by his Mather wen he wus one year old because She wus not married so She could not mange to look after him.

So he had to make his Home in the Orphans Home.

In the Orphans there were rooms for boys andǥ gorls between the age of one and four.

When they became four years of age they go to the boys ward. Ther they had four rooms with (30) boys in each room mokiln-gthr total (120) boys who he could play with.

I

CHAPTER TWO

CHILDHOOD

When he became (six) years of age he made friends with most of the boys and one day his mother came to see him.
The day that his mother came to see him wus the first time that She withkin (five) years so when he saw her he did not know who She wus so to him She wus just a woman who came to take him for a walk to the playgroand and it wus a coincidenee that the day that his mother wanted to see him it wus his birthday and he wus (six ye--ars of age and his mother wus very surprised wan She sew him looking bright for a (six) years old boy.
He used to get up in the mornings at (7 . o Clock and go to the wash room for a wash and after that he would go to the dining room for his breakfast and for breakfast he would have a fried egg and beans followed by bread and batter with a glass of milk.
WHEN HE AS finished his breakfast he would go to the bed rooms to make the beds and sweep the floor by the time he as finished making

CHAPTER THREE

BEFORE THE BOY BECAME (7) YEARS OLD

~~The beds and swept the floor it is (IO). o Clock in the morning~~ and it is time to go to the diningroom for a cip of tea and at (IO.I5) hrs it is time to go to the playground.

In the playground there was sand pits and toys for them to play with if there wont to.

At (I2 o Clock it was time for the boys to go in for dinner and just before dinner he would go to the wash room to wash his hands and just before he washed his hand they are inspected and if his hand are very dirty he is punished.

After dinner at (I2.30) hrs he would go to his bedroom for a rest on his bed till (2 o Clock.

He would aen go and dress in clothes and at (2.30) has he would go for a walk with the rest of the boys and one of the nurses used to go with them.

On the way to the park the nurse would give the boys same sweets and when they get to the park he would play with the swings and

3

PAGE FOUR

---

the duchs on the pond and also play hide-and seek with ~~the~~ the rest of the boys. At (4) o; clock he woud go to the TV room to watch Andy pandy and at (4 15hrs he would go for his tea in the dining room. At (5) o; clock he would go to the TV room and watch TV until (6)o; cjock then he would go to his bedroom and go to bed at 7-30 hrs.

The nurses would take the cup of tea and sandwiches to the boys and after that they would go to the toilet then go to bed to sleep. But not this boy because he was the night nurses pet so he would go to the nurses office and she would talk to him about life and she used to give him sweets.

At (9) o; clock he would go to bed to sleep he would not go to sleep till the nurse gave him a good night kiss.

END CHABTER THREE

CHAPTER FOUR

A BIG SIEP IN HIS LIFE

His mother came to see him when the sister thought he his mother was coming to see him he sed Ido not want to see her because I don;t like her because she is a bad woman and I am going for a walk with nurse welsh and the sister said to him dont be so silty charles your mother has come a long way to see you and he said to the sister again I dont wont to see her.

When his mother came to the Home the sister said to her I am very very sorry Miss but you will not see your son to-day because he is in bed sick and sick patients are not allowed visting and his mother said I have come a long way to see him and I Want to see him the sister did not know whot to do so in the end the went to bed and pretended that he was ill and the sister said to his mother you can see your son for ten minutes.

That visit was the first time his mother said I am your mother son and he said I know you are my mother because you look

PAGE SIX

like me and I look like you and his mother said to him I wish I could take you with me but I cant son and he said to her woy cant ~~you~~ you take me with you and she had no answer.

Visting time was over so his mother said goodbye son for now. The sister went to his bedroom and sat on his bed and told him all about his mother and he said to the sister I would like to go home but I would miss nurse Welsh and the sister said to him you worry like nurse ~~WW~~/ Welsh dont you and he said yes I do sister because she likes me very much and she dont smack me like the these nurses.

THE END OF CHAPTER FOUR

CHAPTER FIVE

THE SISTERS REEPLT NECKST DAY

The sister said to the doctor I think we will have a lhot eg go trouble with because he has a very tunny sense of humour and yester-day his mother came to see ~~hh~~ him and he said to me I do not want to see her.

He said it three time and I said to him dont be so sllty charles but still he said the same but his mother insisted that she would see him.

So when I~~t~~ told him he said I am going to bed and pattient I am ill and I said to him yes that is a good thing to do and Isaid to his mother you can see your son for ten minutes so his mother was very pleased and when she saw him she said I am your mother son and he said Iknow you are my mother because you look like me and ~~Iloo~~ I look like you and his mother said to him you are a very sensible boy son and his mother started to cry and I said to her visting time is over and she said goodbye son.

77/~~/~~

CHAPTER SIX

ONE WEEK LAETER

Nurse Welsh got permission to take him for a holiday with her to Offaly in Iraland.

Now the saturday that Nurse Welsh was going Home the Sister went to the boys ward and said to him Charles would you like to go for a holiday with Nurse Welsh to Iraland and he said yes I would Sister very much indeed and the Sister said to him well Charles you are going with Nurse Welsh to-day if you be a good boy and he said to the Sister O Sister I will be a very very good boy.

So at (I2 O Clock it wus time for dinner but this boy did not want his dinner so he went to his bedroom to get dressed in his best clothes ready for Nurse Welsh to take him home.

BY (2 o clock he wus ready to go and the Sister said to him you look very smart Charles and he said yes Sister I do because Nurse Welsh is coming to take me home and the Sister said

PAGE NINE

Where did you get that shirt from and he said to the Sister Nurse Welsh bouyght it for me to go home with Sister.

At (2.30 hrs Nurse Welsh came to take him home on his holiday.

THE END OC SHAPTER ~~SEVEN~~ Six

THE BEGINNING OF SHAPTER SEVEN

ØØØØØØØØØØØØØØØØØØØØØØØØØØØØØØØ

HOLIDAY IN IEALAND

He said to Nurse Welsh come on Nurse iets go home and they both went to a car and said to the driver take us to the station driver please and the driver said to the boy yes sir and he looked at Nurse Welsh and said I am a sir the driver said.

When he got to the station he had to wait for ten minits then the train came.

PAGE TIN

He got on the train and he said to nurse Welsh I like this train it goes very fast and She said to him yes it goes very fast in-deed and Nurse Welsh had also told him to call her Pat and he said to her Pat why cant I call you Mother and She said to him because I am not your Mother and he said to Pat I know you are not my mother but I wish you was Pat and Pat said to him why do you which I was your mother and he said to her because I like you very very much not like my mother.

When they arrived in Birmingham they had to wait for two hrs to get a train to Liverpool im the meantime they went to a cafe and had a cup of tea and same sandwiches.

Two hrs pass and they both got on the train to Liverpool whre they would get the boats for Ireland.

He had been asleep for some time when the train was slack -ening speed he woke up and he said are we there and Pat said yes we are there Charles all we have to do is to wait for the boat to take us to Ireland but we will wait in a Hotel and see if they ~~ha~~/

PAGE ELEVEN

---

have a bed for us and Charles said to Pat you wont iet me sleep on my own will you and Pat said no I wont Charles we will sleep to-gether in a big bed.

SO they went down the rowd and saw a big hotel and they went to the manager and ~~breakfa/~~ said to the man could we have bed dan breakfast please and the man said madam is it for son and mother and Pat looted at Charles and said yes it is so off they went to the bedroom and the first thing that Charles ~~s~~ said thank you very much for telling the man that Iam your son and kissed Pat on the lips and said I like you very much mam and off they went to bed to sleep.

At (8.30 they got up and went to breakfast after break -fast they went back to the bedroom for (2 hrs then they went to the boat at about (10.30 hrs and the boat would leave at (II00 hrs.

When he got on the boat he said Pat look at the sea mam and Pat did not know whot to say to him because she wished he

II

PAGE TWELVE

---

was her son. When they arrived at pats home Pats mother said hello Pat and pat said hello mum O this is the boy that I told you about the last time Icame home mum and her mother said whot a nice little boy you are and Pat said to him say hello and he said hello Granny and Pat looted at him and he looted up and sa -id to Pats mother you dont mind if I call you Granny do you and Pats mother said no I dont mind at all so Pat takes him to bed to have a rest.

Pat and her mother was siting in the front room tallking about him and Pat said to her mother i wish he was my son and her mother said if he was you would have a very good son Pat but you musint tell him because I can see whot is going to happen so be very careful and Pat said to her mother dont tell my father will you? and her father came home and Pat greeted him with a smile and a kiss and he said where is the boy Pat and she said he is in bed and as Pat said bed the boy came down the stairs and said hello and Pats father said hello how are you and he page thirteen

said I am well thank you very much Pats father picked him up and cuddled him and Pat looted at her mother I and said I dont know whot to do so her mother said jet us have so tea.

When thet were having their tea Pat said to Charles affer tea we will go to miss and thank god for his holiday that he has given us and he said yes we must thank god mom for this holiday.

So when tea was over Pats father went to his room and put his best suit on ready for mass and Charles said to him Grandpa are you coming to mass and he said yes I am son.

So off they went to mass and Charles was very hoppy that Pats mother and father went to mass with him in fackt he said to Pat I like you mom and dad very very much indeed.

As they workt up the street Pat could see the Charch and Pat said to Charles there is the Charch and he said to

PAGE FOURTEEN

Pat I like your mom and dad very much indeed.

As they walked up the street Pat could see the Church and Pat said to Charles look there is the Church and he said to Pat yes I can see it mom and when they got to the Church Charles said O; what a big Charch.

So mass was over and they all go home and have a cup of tea and a bun after supper Charles was sleepy so they all went off to bed at Nine O; clock it had been a long day for Pat and Charles.

Next morning at (8.30 hrs Charles gets up and looks out the winddw and he could see a horse and a man and when he went down*~~stairs~~ stairs to the kitchen he said I saw a horse with a man and Pats mother said to him come~~d~~ and have you breakfast son and after breakfast you can go out to play with the boys and gorls and he sa where is mom she is gone to the shops son.

SO after breakfast he went out to plat with the

PAGE FIFTEEN

boys and girls and when Pat was getting off the bus he said to the boys and girls their is my mom coming up the rowd i am going home and when Pat got hom the time was (I0.30 hrs and Charles said hello mom whet have you been doing and he sa -id I have been playing with the boys and girls and Pat said to her mother has he been a good boy and Pats mother said yes he has been a very good indeed but he was very worried about you Pat when he got up this morring the very thing he said was where is Pat?

It was a good holiday but it soon ended and he was on his way back to Pewsey

THE END OF CHAPTER SEVEN

I5

PAGE SIXTEEN

CHAPTER EIGHT

HE WAS BACK IN PEWSEY

When he arrived at the home his mother was wating for him to come back from his holiday and take him for a walk but by the time he arrived visiting time was over and he was very glad too because he did not wont to see his mother as he ignored her after his holiday with Pat and he did hot went it spoiled but the Sister said to him your mother is coming to see you nrxt saturday.

One week later his mother came to see him and she said to the SIster is my son back and she said yes Miss your son is back and you can see him I will take you to him and his mother said thank you very much indeed.

When she got to the visiting room his mother said to the sister who is Nurse Welsh and what is she like and the sister said she is very kind person and she is the best Nurse I have got and to the boys she is very kind and especially to your son

PAGE SEVENTEEN

Miss and his mother said can I see her and the sister said yes you can Iwill go and tell her that you would like to see her and I am sure that she will be delighted to see you and the sister said to Nurse Welsh Charies ;s mother would like to see you Nurse and she said to the sister where is she nad the Sister said she is in the visiting room .

SO Nurse welsh went to see his mother and on her way there she saw the Doctor and he said to her where are you go -ing to see Charles ;s mother because the ~~Sistner~~ Sister said that she would like to meet me and he said be very careful whot you say to her wont you,? yes I will sir so of she webt to see his mother and when she saw his mother she said hello miss how are you? and his mother replyed all right thankyou very much Nurse.

So you are the Nurse that took my son for a Holiday and before she could say yes Charles said yes and she is my

PAGE EIGHTEEN

mother now so I dont need you to visit me any more and his mot -her said to Nures Welsh now look whot you have done to my son you have turned my son awayfrom me and Nurse said dont be so silly Miss   I was only trying to help him and if you were a good mother you would take him home with you and give him the bast home you think he deserved and believe me you would have to give him a lot too but if you went take him home with you I will see the Docter and see if I can get a home for him and his mother said you cant do that because I am his mother and before you do that you will have to get my cinsent and I will not let you do it so dont think I am mad Nurse ~~and~~ and Nurse Welsh said well Miss   I am going to say one more time if you dont take him home it will be a shame and a good boy is going to wayst as Nurse WElsh said wayst Charse looed up ans said I am fed up mom take me to the playgroand and his mother said wait a minute and hr said I dont want you I want my new mom to

PAGE NINETEEN

take me to the playgroand and his mother looed at him and said if you dont be a good boy I will tan your bottom and he said you wont because my mom wont let you and he said that mother smacked him on the face and Nurse Welsh said to her there was no need of that Miss   I will see the Doctor in the morning and he said again please go to the playgroand please mom and she said no you say with you mother son I dont went to and he ran out the door to the sister ans she said where is your mother Charlse and he said she is in the visiting room with Nursa Welsh and Nurse is going to see the Docter in the morning about my mother because she smacked my face and the sister went to the visiting room to see his mother ans when she arrived there she said to Nurse Welsh I have just seen Charlse and he said to me that his mother smacked his face is that so.

Nurse Welsh said yse sister that is so and the sister said Miss   I will put this in my reeport.

I9

PAGE TWENTY

His mother said to the sister I dont think it is your business what Ido to my son sister and the sister said to her Miss

I think you are a very silly woman and I will see the Docter at (5 o; clock and tell him what has happened and I dont think the Docter will permit you to see him any more and she said you can not stop me seeing my son so there.

THE END OF CHAPTER EIGHT

20

PAGE TWENTY)ONE

CHAPTER NINE

ONE YEAR PAST

On his ninth Birthday he was sent to West Stone it was a home for boys and girls between ~~hn~~ the age/of nine and twelve.
When he arrived at his new home he was very pleased as he had sent by the Doctor because he was very intelligent and very brainy.

At West Stone the boys and girls used to get up at (8 o; clock in the morning and at (9 o; clock they would go to the dinning room for there breakfast and after he would go to the toy room for his toys and then he would go to the playgroand with/the boys and girld.

But to him it was just the same as Pewsey Hospital. Next morning the Doctor came to visit/t the boys and girls and he said to Charles how are you

PAGE TWENTY-TWO

Charles at your new home and he said to the Doctor it is just the same as Pewsey Hospital Doctor and he said whot do you mean Charles" and he said to him well I dont know how to explain but I will try and explain to you Doctor.

Well it is like this it this home I dont go to School and I cant read or write Doctor and the Doctor said to him would you like to gp to school and he said yes I would very very much and the Doctor said to him I will see whot I can do for you son and he said to the Doctor thank you very much indeed I will all ways remember what you said to mr and the Doctor said to him I can't promise you that I will send you to School but I will promise you one think I will see whot I can do for you son.

So off he went to the toy room and he said to one of the boys I may be going to School soon I have just been to see the Doctor and hr said to me I will see whot I cane do for you and the boy said I will go and see the Doctor and see if I can go with

22

PAGE TWENTY-THREE

you Terracne and Terracne" said to Sam how do you know my name was Terracne and Sam said because I was told and Terracne said to SAm my real Name is Terracne Charles and Sam said to Charles my real Name is Sam Dabld .

Sam was one year older then Charles and he was his best friend and they all ways would be to gether when they go out to play.

But one day Charles made friends with a girl and Sam was very very jules because Charles made friends with a girl and the girls Name was Susan and she was a very pretty girl too Charles said to Sam you are jules Sam becaues she dont like you and Sam said to Charles I"m not jules and Charles said yes you are Sam" and SAm jumped up and hit Charles and Charles' said now I know you are jules and if you hit me once more I will hit you back Sam so Sam hit Charles and Charles' said rite I am going to hit you and Charles him him so hard he started to cry and

PAGE TWENTY-FOUR

Susan said dont hit him Charles because he is cring like a baby and Charles said yes Sam is a baby.

Susan said to Charles lets go to the playground and he said yes that is a good ideer Susan and of they went to the playground.

THE END OF CHAPTER NINE

PAGE TWENTY-FIVE

CHAPTER TEN

THE NEXS DAY

The Sister said to Sam whot did Charles hit you for and Sam said I dont know Sister and the Sister said to Sam go and tell Charles I want to see him and Sam said yes I will go and tell him and Sam went to the toy room and he said to Charles

the Sister wants to seeyou and Charles said where is she and he said in her office and Charles said to Sam thank jules for telling me.

So off Charles went to see the Sister and when they said to him whot did you hit Sam for and Charles said to the Sister the reeson I hit him is because he hit me and I said to him if you hit me once more I will hit you and he hit me so I hit him and ~~more~~/~~and~~/ he started to cry so I did not him him any more and Susan also tell me not to hit him any more and the Sister said to him is this true Charles and Charles said yes

25

PAGE TWENTY-SIX

Sister it is and the Sister said thank you very muck Charles I will see Sam and tell him that he is a bad boy thank you Sister but dont sackn him will you because he is my best pal and the Sister said no I wont sack him Charles thank you Sister.

Two hrs layter Sam said to Charles" Charles I am very very sorry for hitting you and whot you said to me is because Susan is the truth and I am very jealous because I like Susan too but you are my best pal and Susan is your girl friend and Charles said yes you are my best pal and Susan is my girl friend and I like her very much Sam and Sam said she is a very pretty girl Charles and Charles said I know she is pretty and she is very nice too.

Susan said to Charles to you want to go out to play and he said yes Susan I would so off they went to the play -ground and Charles said to Susan" Susan Sam said to me that he like you and I am his bast pal but I dont need him as I have got

26

Note: This is the extent of the autobiographical text available.

Bibliography

Anthony, G. "Cerebral Dominance as an Etiological Factor in Dyslexia." Ph.D. dissertation, New York University, 1968.

Blanchard, P. "Reading Disabilities in Relation to Maladjustment." *Mental Hygiene* 12 (1928): 772–88.

Bond, G. L., and Tinker, M. A. *Reading Difficulties—Their Diagnosis and Correction.* New York: Appleton-Century-Crofts, 1967.

Bowlby, J., et al. "Effects of Mother-Child Separation: a Follow-up Study." *British Journal of Medical Psychology* 29 (1956): 221–47.

Bowley, A. H. *A Handbook on the Care of the Child Deprived of Normal Home Life.* Edinburgh: Livingstone, 1951.

Bradshaw, F. "Remedial Work in School." Chapter 13 in *Childhood Problems and the Teacher*, edited by C. Buhler. London: Routledge and Kegan Paul, 1953.

Brennan, W. K. "A Policy for Remedial Education." *Remedial Education* 6 (1971): 7–13.

Burt, C. *The Backward Child.* London: University of London Press, 1937.

———. *The Subnormal Mind.* Oxford: Oxford University Press, 1955.

———. "Recent Studies of Abilities and Attainment." *Journal of the Association of Educational Psychologists* 2, no. 4 (1969): 4–9.

Castle, M. "Institution and Non-Institution Children at School." *Journal of Human Relations* 7 (1954).

Cleugh, M. F. *The Slow Learner—Some Educational Principles and Policies.* London: Methuen, 1968.

Cole, R. *Comprehensive Schools in Action.* London: Oldbourne, 1964.

Coville, W. J.; Costello, T. W.; and Rouke, F. L. *Abnormal Psychology.* New York: Barnes and Noble, 1960.

Department of Education and Science. *Progress in Reading, 1948–64.* Education Pamphlet No. 50. London: H.M.S.O., 1966.

Downing, J. A. "i.t.a.'s Effectiveness in the Prevention and Treatment of Disabilities in Reading and Writing." Paper presented at the World Mental Health Congress, Washington, D.C., 1969.

Downing, J. A., and Gardner, K. "New Experimental Evidence on the Role of Unsystematic Spelling of English in Reading Failure." *Educational Research* 5 (1962): 69–76.

Faris, R. E. L. "Ecological Factors in Human Behavior." In *Personality and the Behavior Disorders*, vol. 2, edited by J. McV. Hunt. New York: Ronald Press, 1944.

Farley, R. *Secondary Modern Discipline*. London: Black, 1960.
Ferguson, C. F. *The Young Delinquent in His Social Setting: A Glasgow Study*. Oxford: Oxford University Press, 1952.
Fernald, G. M. *Remedial Techniques in Basic School Subjects*. New York: McGraw-Hill, 1943.
Fraser, E. D. *Home Environment and the School*. London: University of London Press, 1959.
Freeman, H. E., and Showell, M. "The Role of the Family in the Socialization Process." Journal of Social Psychology 37 (1955): 97–101.
Gardner, K. "The State of Reading." In *Crisis in the Classroom*. London: Hamlyn, 1968.
Gates, A. I. "The Role of Personality Maladjustment in Reading Ability." *Journal of Genetic Psychology* 59 (1941): 77–83.
Gates, A. I., and Bond, G. L. "Relation of Handedness, Eye-sighting and Acuity Dominance to Reading." *Journal of Educational Psychology* 27 (1936): 450–456.
Goodacre, E. J. *Provision for Reading*. Reading, Eng.: Reading University, 1971.
Hargreaves, D. M. *Social Relations in a Secondary School*. London: Routledge and Kegan Paul, 1967.
Harrison, M. *Instant Reading: The Story of the Initial Teaching Alphabet*. London: Pitman, 1968.
Holmes, J. A. "Emotional Factors and Reading Disabilities." *The Reading Teacher* 9 (1955): 11–17.
Inner London Education Authority. *Interim Literacy Survey*. 1969.
Jones, E. *The Treatment of the Neuroses*. London: Balliere, Tindall and Cox, 1920.
Kemp, L. C. D. "Environmental and Other Characteristics Determining Attainments in Primary Schools." *British Journal of Educational Psychology* 25 (1955): 67–71.
MacMeeken, M. *Developmental Aphasia in Educationally Retarded Children*. London: University of London Press, 1942.
Mannheim, H., and Wilkins, L. T. *Prediction Methods in Relation to Borstal Training*. London: H.M.S.O., 1955.
Mays, J. B. *Growing up in the City: A Study of Juvenile Delinquency in an Urban Neighbourhood*. Liverpool: Liverpool University Press, 1954.
Mazurkiewicz, A. J. "The Initial Teaching Alphabet." In *The Disabled Reader*, edited by J. Money. Baltimore: Johns Hopkins University Press, 1966.
Ministry of Education. *Reading Ability*. Pamphlet No. 18. London: H.M.S.O., 1950.
———. *15 to 18* (*The Crowther Report*), 2 vols. London: H.M.S.O., 1960.
———. *Half Our Future* (*The Newsom Report*). London: H.M.S.O., 1963.
———. *Children and Their Primary Schools* (*The Plowden Report*). London: H.M.S.O., 1967.
Monroe, M. *Children Who Cannot Read*. Chicago: University of Chicago Press, 1932.
Morris, J. M. *Standards and Progress in Reading*. Slough: National Foundation for Educational Research, 1966.

National Association for Remedial Education. *Adult Illiteracy*. Stafford, Eng.: National Association for Remedial Education, 1972.

National Child Development Survey. *11,000 Seven-Year-Olds*. London: Longman, 1966.

Nisbet, J. D. "Family Environment: A Direct Effect of Family Size on Intelligence." In *Occasional Papers on Eugenics*, No. 8. London: Cassell, 1953.

Optical Information Research Council. *A Random Survey of 1,000 School Children*. London: Optical Information Research Council, 1968.

Parson, B. S. *Left-handedness—A New Interpretation*. New York: Macmillan, 1924.

Peters, M. L. "The Influence of Reading Methods on Spelling." *British Journal of Educational Psychology* 37 (1967): 47–53.

Platt, G. Data collected for a proposed M.Ed. thesis, University of Manchester, 1971.

Pringle, M. L. K., and Bossio, V. "A Study of Deprived Children: Part I, Intellectual, Emotional and Social Development." *Vita Humana* 1 (1958): 65–92.

Riesman, D. *The Lonely Crowd*. New Haven: Yale University Press, 1950.

Robinson, M. M. *Why Pupils Fail in Reading*. Chicago: University of Chicago Press, 1946.

Schonell, F. J. *Backwardness in the Basic Subjects*. Edinburgh: Oliver & Boyd, 1942.

Schools Council. *Society and the Young School Leaver*. Working Paper No. 11. London: Schools Council, 1967.

———. "The Individual in Society," H. T. Himmelweit. Working Paper No. 12. In *The Educational Implications of Social and Economic Change*, pp. 13–20. London: H.M.S.O., 1967.

Sherman, M. "Emotional Disturbances and Reading Disability." In *Recent Trends in Reading*, edited by William S. Gray. Supplementary Educational Monographs, No. 49. Chicago: University of Chicago Press, 1939.

Siegel, M. "The Personality Structure of Children with Reading Disabilities as Compared with Children Presenting Other Clinical Problems." *The Nervous Child* 10, nos. 3–4 (1954): 409–14.

Smith, N. "Therapy as Part of Remedial Education." *The Reading Teacher* 9 (1955): 18–23.

Southgate, V. *Reading and the Language Arts*. Submission to the James Committee's Inquiry into Teacher Training, 1971.

Start, K. B., and Wells, B. K. *The Trend of Reading Standards*. Slough: National Foundation for Educational Research, 1972.

Taylor, E. A. *Experiments with a Backward Class*. London: Methuen, 1949.

Thrasher, F. M. *The Gang*. Chicago: University of Chicago Press, 1927.

Trenaman, J. *Out of Step*. London, Methuen, 1952.

Trieschman, R. B. "Undifferentiated Handedness and Perceptual Development in Children with Reading Problems." *Perceptual and Motor Skills* 27 (1968): 1123–34.

Tyerman, M. *Truancy*. London: University of London Press, 1958.

Veness, T. *School Leavers*. London: Methuen, 1962.

Vernon, P. E. *Intelligence and Attainment Tests*. London: University of London Press, 1960.

———. *Structure of Human Abilities.* London: Methuen, 1961.

Wall, W. D. "Reading Backwardness Among Men in the Army." *British Journal of Educational Psychology* 15 (1946): 28–40; 16 (1946): 133–48.

———. *Adolescents in School and Society.* Slough: National Foundation for Educational Research, 1968.

Warburton, F. W. "Attainment and the School Environment." Chapter 6 in *Education and Environment*, edited by S. Wiseman. Manchester: Manchester University Press, 1968.

Warburton, F. W., and Southgate, V. *i.t.a.—An Independent Evaluation.* London: Murray, 1969.

White, Col. A. C. T., VC. *The Story of Army Education.* London: Harrap, 1963.

Wiseman, S. *Education and Environment.* Manchester: Manchester University Press, 1968.

Witty, P., and Kopel, D. *Reading and the Educative Process.* Boston: Ginn, 1939.

Wood, B. D., and Freeman, F. *An Experimental Study of the Educational Influences of the Typewriter in the Elementary School Classroom.* New York: Macmillan, 1932.

Wright, M. "Letter to the Editor." *Times Educational Supplement*, October 29, 1971.

Zangwill, O. L. "Dyslexia in Relation to Cerebral Dominance." In *Reading Disability: Progress and Research Needs in Dyslexia*, edited by J. Money. Baltimore: Johns Hopkins University Press, 1962.

About The Author

COLIN STEVENSON was born in Newburgh, Lancashire, United Kingdom. He was educated at the universities of London and Southampton. He followed a military career in the Royal Army Educational Corps for 23 years during which time he gradually became a specialist in the fields of learning disabilities, brain damage, and emotional disorders in adults.

He has visited the United States as an adviser to the U.S. Department of Defense and to universities and state education departments. He was awarded the Bronze Medallion and Citation of the Educational Records Bureau of the United States for distinguished services to education.

Mr. Stevenson was involved in the submission of evidence to the U.K. Bullock Committee of Inquiry into Reading and the Teaching of English and to the Warnock Committee on Special Educational Needs. He was a member of the Working Party set up by the British Council for Rehabilitation of the Disabled, which produced the report *People with Dyslexia*. Resulting from this, he left the Army in 1974 and was appointed Director of the Learning Disability Centre of the British Council for Rehabilitation of the Disabled, now the Royal Association for Disability and Rehabilitation.

In 1980 he was appointed Director of the Learning Disabilities Unit at the University of Southampton.

Index

Italicized numbers refer to pages on which tables are located.